T. Scott Gross

Millennial Rules

How to connect
with the first
digitally savvy
generation
of consumers
and employees

ALLWORTH PRESS
NEW YORK

D0967392

17 16 15 14 13 5 4 3 2 1

Published by Allworth Press, an imprint of Skyhorse Publishing, Inc. 307 West 36th Street, 11th Floor, New York, NY 10018.

Allworth Press® is a registered trademark of Skyhorse Publishing, Inc.®, a Delaware corporation.

www.allworth.com

Interior design by Jenn Taylor
Cover design by Mary Belibasakis

Library of Congress Cataloging-in-Publication Data is available on file.

Print ISBN: 978-1-62153-423-5
Ebook ISBN: 978-1-62153-420-4

Printed in the United States of America

ACKNOWLEDGMENTS

I write about what interests me. Trust me, if I'm not having fun writing a book, you aren't going to have much fun reading it. Good news! I had a ball working on this one!

It's too bad that it isn't possible to list everyone who helped with this book. Without exception, whenever I called for help, the answer was always "Yes!" A man can't have better friends.

Fred Vang was my first call because Fred is, in my mind, the world's greatest salesman. Fred truly loves his customers. Never has a salesperson gone to such lengths to be absolutely certain that he is delivering a perfect match of customer and product.

When I need first-class research, I am blessed to work with my friends at BIGinsight™. I can count on Gary Drenik, Phil Rist, Chrissy Wissinger, and the rest of the gang to answer my most esoteric questions. They and their remarkable company deliver a look into the future with an accuracy that is almost spooky. If you are running a business in these turbulent times, you would be nuts not to have them as a vendor partner.

And then there is my friend Bill Wagner of Accord Management Systems. Bill knows more about matching people to the work at hand than anyone on the planet. If you are hiring staff or qualifying dealers or franchisees, I wouldn't take a chance of doing it without Bill's expertise. Whenever I have called on Bill, his only response has been, "How can I help?"

A huge thank you goes to Tim Durkin, a very smart and cool guy for all his help with the Culture Calculator.

And last but never least is Buns, my wife, business partner, and best friend for nearly four decades. Who would have imagined? I gave her well over 100,000 words, and she gave me back something much, much shorter (and a much different book than I had written). Go figure! I hate to think of all the neat stuff that is now languishing on a hard drive in the closet. Maybe it will be the heart of another book . . . who knows?

TABLE OF CONTENTS

Foreword ix

Introduction: Millennials and the Cursive Code 1

    Is Your Tail on Fire? 2

    Caution: Trends Ahead 4

    How I Learned to Love Millennials 5

PART ONE : A NEW GENERATION 9

Chapter 1: The Digital Consumer 11

    What Makes a Generation? 12

    Appreciate the Good News 17

    Don't Bucket 20

Chapter 2: Portrait of a Millennial 21

    My Way, Right Away, Why Pay? 21

    Technology Rules 22

    Social Media Matters 24

    Timing Is Everything 25

    Everything Is Negotiable 25

    Sales Expectations Are Soaring 26

    Millennials at Work 31

    Millennials at Home 33

    Action Steps 35

    Your New Customer 37

PART TWO: THE MESSAGE FROM MILLENNIALS 43

Chapter 3: "Don't *Sell* Me Anything" 45

    Become Invisible 45

    Light the Sales FUSE 49

    Create a Positive Feeling 54

Chapter 4: "I'm Not Afraid of Technology" 59

    Use Technology to Become Invisible 60

    Understand and Meet the New Expectations 60

    Do It Right 61

    Use Networks 62

    Don't Forget about Traditional Marketing 63

Chapter 5: "I Live through Social Media" 67
    Understand the Power of Social Media 69
    Market with Social Media 73
    Grow the Program 77
    Spread the Word 78
    Have a Conversation 79

Chapter 6: "I Want It My Way" 81
    Expect Prepurchase Research 81
    Deliver Options 84
    Prepare to Negotiate 85
    Unbundle Your Service 86
    Don't Make Them Wait 88
    Remember the Critical Service Points 88

Chapter 7: "Surprise Me" 91
    Deliver Positively Outrageous Service 91
    Treat Me Right When Things Go Wrong 98
    Make Me Laugh 100

Chapter 8: "Train Me, but Don't Constrain Me" 103
    Meet the New Employee 105
    Understand the New Values 107
    Hire Great People 111
    Train Your People 114
    Measure Success 120
    Recognize the Benefits 121

PART THREE: THE CRYSTAL BALL 123

Chapter 9: What's Next? 125
    The Path to Progress 125
    The Future of Employees 126
    The Future of Customer Service 129
    A Play-by-Play Peek Ahead 130
    Some Things Never Change 131

PART FOUR: THINGS YOU SHOULD HAVE LEARNED AT
            HOME . . . BUT PROBABLY DIDN'T! 133

Chapter 10: As the Saying Goes 135
    Why Millennials Need Rules 136
    Leading the Under-Class 137

Chapter 11: The Boss as Parent 141
    The Millennial Rules 142
Notes 151
Bibliography 153
Index 157
About the Author 163

FOREWORD

Just about the time you think you have things all figured out . . . you don't. Like when I wrote *Positively Outrageous Service*, I figured I had written the definitive work on customer service. I was close but as every author knows, there's always more.

I haven't managed to write this book all the way from beginning to end without experiencing my first twinge of "Oh, crap!" Only this time I am not going to worry about it. After more than a dozen books I have finally chilled to the thought that this is a good sign. It means I had been thinking; it means that you will be thinking too. And that's what a good book should do—get you thinking.

So let me grab a thought I had with only a few pages to go. Maybe it is more accurate to say that a generation is defined as a sticking place of sorts. We are born, we grow into our sticking place and through no more than the luck of the draw we find ourselves defined more by circumstance than genetics.

No matter how you define yourself and those who are sharing your ride on this good, old planet Earth, keep in mind that you don't have to be stuck. As matter of fact, you don't have to be anything. It's a choice. And that's the best Millennial rule if ever there was one!

Millennials and the Cursive Code

I t had been a digital day. My digital day started when I punched the keypad (digital) to open the garage door. The digital display on my bike showed 82 degrees, and it was not yet 6:30 a.m. As I rode down the street, I looked toward my grandkids' house and chuckled over the idea that an old-fashioned analog clock would be tough for them to read.

After my ride, I grabbed the newspaper on the way back into the house and couldn't help noticing how few houses in my neighborhood had a newspaper waiting on their front lawn. Not to worry; I could see an upstairs light on in the neighbor's house, a sure sign that Joe was awake and reading the paper online.

Back in my kitchen, I spotted a thank-you note our eighteen-year-old grandson had left on the counter. His neat printing gave away the fact that he is a Millennial. To him and the rest of his demographic cohort, cursive writing is as good as secret code.

As I opened the local paper, I was surprised to see I had been featured in an article on "digital seniors." I knew I was digital but never thought of myself as a senior, being just over sixty. *Senior* is for old people, not me! Still, I realized my grandson didn't wonder what had happened to thermometers filled with shiny but toxic mercury, watches with or without hands, cameras with eight millimeter film, and television sets with vacuum tubes and knobs labeled "horizontal hold." Though we are both digitally savvy, his generation doesn't remember any of these things. I shook my head, finished my reading, and spent the rest of the morning in my office surrounded by my digital toys.

Later that day, I drove into town for a city council meeting to review the plans for a new city hall. In spite of our careful planning, I suspected our new structure would be obsolete the day we opened its doors. Several years earlier, we had built our dream house in the Texas hill country. I had prematurely congratulated myself for having the foresight to install category 5 wiring only to discover that the world had gone wireless in the time it took to finish the house. I didn't know what surprises technology would have for our city project, but I was certain there would be something unexpected.

When the architect unveiled the artist's renderings of the new city hall, if you looked closely, you could see that one of the figures walking across the still-imagined campus was wearing a short-sleeved t-shirt and a knit cap pulled completely over his ears. I jokingly said to the architect, "I see our new city hall campus comes complete with slackers."

"Oh, we've got some young people in the art department," he said. "I guess they were just having fun."

Well, those young people, just having fun, are about to take over the world—so the rest of us had better figure them out. Don't worry; they are smart and creative, and they seem to have their priorities straight. Best of all, they are amazingly tolerant of old people. (If you're one of them, thanks for that!)

Besides, if you want to fool with them, you can always leave them a note in cursive.

Is Your Tail on Fire?

Change is interesting or scary, depending on your personality. It's also inevitable.

My grandmother taught me about change. She died about thirty years before she quit breathing. For the last several decades of her life, she didn't try different food, sample new ideas, or let technology encroach on her life if she could avoid it. For the last thirty years, she only took up space.

The last thing I want is to be seen as an old guy who has stayed too long at the party. So I try to stay on the leading edge rather than play catch up. I try to live by the motto, "If you aren't living on the edge, you are taking up too much space." Or, as pilots like to say, "Live like your tail is on fire!"

That's the way Millennials live—like their tails are on fire. They aren't going to trade their freedom to enjoy life for a comfortable corner office. Millennials are going to live until they die.

Some say we are about to enter a perfect storm of change, but really, we're already in the storm. Technology is advancing exponentially, and that means a digital generation has come of age while a generation of Boomers still clings to the executive washroom key. It is going to be a struggle of epic and historic proportions.

That brings us to the idea behind *Millenial Rules*. As we'll see, research tells us that old-fashioned ideas of selling, serving, and marketing are going to need tweaking—or perhaps even a total overhaul. Customer service is changing, too. Today's consumer is more informed (thanks to the Internet) and isn't shy about negotiating. More surprising is the discovery that when customers want help, they want it *now*; but when they *don't* want help, they expect the sales staff to be invisible. These consumers have learned to think of customer service as a separate product that can be negotiated. They are increasingly comfortable being served by avatars and outsourced human customer service representatives. Finally, old ideas of marketing aren't going to work in this new age of social media. Yes, you can still market to your customers, but in the new age, the best marketing is going to be invisible.

In the following pages, you're going to learn about the Millennials and how they are impacting the older generations (Gen X, Boomers, and Traditionals). The Millennials are changing the way things get done and goods get sold. Older generations may interpret their approach as radical, but for the most part Millennials are simply finishing the job on changes that older, perhaps more cautious generations didn't have the courage to complete. There is much to learn from these new kids on the block, this odd collection of tattoos, piercings, and scared hair. Millennials represent the bulk of the most amazing generation of all, the first generation to conduct its social interactions via digital communications.

Does this mean the members of the old guard are slowly turning in their keys, heading into the sunset? No. They aren't, and that's one of the things that make our time so darned interesting. In spite of new technology, certain basic traits of human nature are still appreciated: storytelling, intimacy, and the joy of being pleasantly surprised. And although we're taking a lot of time to learn how to sell to Millennials, we'll end up doing a better job of selling and serving everyone else, too! Differences are fun to point out, but in the end, you will see that much of what we see as differences is really nothing more than a matter of context.

Caution: Trends Ahead

Trend spotting is not what it used to be. In the not-so-distant past, you could spot a trend from a mile away. Life today is changing so rapidly that the vantage point moves closer by the hour. The trends we spotlight here are not a mile away; they are upon us now. And if we don't react quickly, we are bound to get run over by our competition. To benefit from these trends, you must do the following:

- Provide a service or product that can survive unbundling (something that is "worth it" on its own).

- Be willing to personalize and customize like never before.

- Market where your customers are.

- Be proficient at recruiting, training, and leading a team of Millennials.

- Do all of the preceding better and more efficiently than your competition.

- Spread a little joy in the form of what we call Positively Outrageous Service (POS). You'll get the full definition of Positively Outrageous Service in chapter 7, but for now, let's just say that POS is service that makes you say "wow!"

In later chapters, we will discuss the how-tos. We will go deep on how to sell and serve, but when it comes to quality and price, we can only share customers' opinions as to how your business measures up. With this base of information, it is up to you whether you rise or fall.

How I Learned to Love Millennials

A few words about some things you will find frequently in this book.

One is what I refer to as "the research." Like the product of the 1960s that I am, I began this project as I have done so many times before—I headed to the public library. But like the New Age person I would like to be, I prepped for my library visits by repeated visits to Amazon.com. Amazon has become the modern-day equivalent of the card catalog. I skimmed books by the dozen, Googled constantly, and read blogs until they became a blur to see what others had to say about the subject; there's no point in writing a book that has already been written. My ultimate gut check came from blogging about my Millennial discoveries, and best of all, I conducted focus groups and impromptu interviews.

The actual research, much to my surprise, already had its foundation in the research I did in cooperation with BIGinsight for a book we cowrote, *When Customers Talk*. For that book, we polled just shy of ten thousand online consumers every month for forty-eight months and accumulated more than twelve million data points. When we re-sorted for generation cohorts, a ton of valuable information suddenly appeared as if by magic. We followed up with even more surveying pointed directly at the Millennials.

But my favorite research didn't begin until I had an attitude change. It's human nature to dismiss, avoid, or fear people and things that are different, and like my grandparents and yours, I had tossed all young people into the same box. Old people had taught me to shake my head and say, "Kids these days . . ."

Stop right there. Kids these days are as different one from another as their generation is different from the ones that preceded. If you want to get to know them, you have to talk to them. And that's what I did and will continue to do. That's also how I came to the conclusion that the Millennials are likely to become the most influential generation ever.

The most fun and thought-provoking research has been in the form of focus groups. I'll continue doing them at every opportunity. In a focus group, abetted by the dynamics of a small group, you pick up nuances. And Millennials will answer any question you are bold enough to ask. Killer!

I also want to introduce here a few key players you will meet time and again.

One of the really cool things about writing a book is that it is a built-in excuse for authors to call just about anybody, all in the name of research. It's also an invitation for readers to establish relationships with authors. And that's pretty much how I met Fred Vang. Fred was an early adopter of my first book, *Positively Outrageous Service.* One conversation led to another and eventually to what has become a cherished friendship. It turned out that Fred is the greatest salesperson on the planet. He has become my mentor when it comes to serving through sales.

There is another key player who by nature hangs in the background. That's my wife, Buns. If you ask me how she acquired that moniker, I plead the Fifth. If you ask her, she is likely to smile and say, "It's all behind me now!" Buns sees herself as a support person. I see her as a smart and energetic partner.

While it's not my nature to talk about myself, I need to give you enough background information to establish my street cred.

I grew up in the restaurant business, starting as a dishwasher at age eleven. In those days, dishes were washed by hand in four-compartment sinks. The last compartment was heated by a gas burner until the water was hot enough to boil a lobster (or an eleven-year-old boy). But I loved it.

Now, if you asked me, "What is your favorite job?" I would probably say that the best job in the world is a breakfast cook at Denny's. It got me through college, and it taught me that you can learn quite a bit about life when you are paying your own way.

Along the way, I have owned two restaurants, worked as a corporate training director, and served six years on the local school board, as well as three two-year terms on city council. I have championed a few projects that make our town a great place to live, and I am proud to say I never let the next election influence my vote.

Somewhere along the line, I was asked to speak about what I call Positively Outrageous Service. It became the first of what are now fourteen books. I speak to audiences of all sizes just about anywhere you can find a quiet spot. While researching my other books, I became a certified wildland firefighter, an instrument-rated pilot, and an EMT. I also became an incurable storyteller.

(And, just to be candid, I have Parkinson's, but Parkinson's doesn't have me.)

I have a truly wonderful and successful son, a beautiful, hand-picked daughterette, two wonderful grandkids, and of course, Buns, the greatest love a man could have.

I started this project with few preconceived notions other than those gained naturally through employing Millennials by the dozen. One of our endeavors was a family-oriented sports-themed restaurant. Millennials are my people . . . I love them! And you will, too, as you first get to know them, then as the book unfolds, learn how to serve and sell to them. Read on!

PART ONE
A New Generation

CHAPTER 1

The Digital Consumer

The Great Recession of the early twenty-first century was an event masquerading as a trend. Hidden within the unemployment and foreclosure statistics were signs of a fundamental change in the way our economy operates. If we had been watching closely, we might have recognized the vanguard of a completely new kind of customer—the digital consumer.

The agency of record for this new consumer is the Millennials, also known as Generation Y. There are good reasons why I have elected to feature the Millennials; after all, they're the ones who will exert the greatest influence on the direction this world is going to go—but they are not the only players, not by a long shot. The other customers are still around: Generation X, the Boomers, the Traditionals.

Who are they? For those of you who live by numbers, let's begin with a rudimentary definition based on age. There's a lot more to it, of course, but this is a place to start.

- **Generation Y**—People born after 1980
- **Generation X**—People born between 1965 and 1980
- **Boomers**—People born between 1946 and 1964
- **Traditionals**—People born before 1946

Folks who were born after 1975 have never lived in an analog world. For our purposes, I tack on a few years of Gen X (1975–1980) to the tail of Gen Y and call this group *Millennials*.

So the digital consumer, the one we all have to learn to understand, is an amalgamation of a little bit Gen X and a lot Gen Y—that is, if we're speaking strictly about age, which is not always the smart thing to do.

The Digital Age was well underway when the first Millennial made an appearance. Gen X was just coming of age, and if you don't mind me saying so, we Boomers were not what you would call over the hill. The point? In spite of a wide range in age, more than one generation has shared in the growth of our digital lifestyle.

Recently, I went to the tire store with my mother to help her pick out a set of new tires. The clerk was fast, friendly, and clearly well trained. Writing up the purchase order, the young man asked for Mom's street address. "There's no need for that," she answered. "If you need me, call my cell or drop me an email." Mom, nearly eighty, shows all the signs of a Millennial.

There is but one key to admission into the Millennial generation: technology, specifically digital technology.

What Makes a Generation?

We used to have a rule of thumb that a generation is twenty-five years. I learned that in third grade in Covington, Kentucky, but I don't buy it anymore. Today I believe a generation is determined by the values and experiences of your most formative years. (For me, that was the 1960s.) And I believe that music is also a big factor. To my way of thinking, those are the things that count: values, experiences, and music.

Being a Boomer, I firmly believe the best music is from the 1960s. My son is Gen X. For years I've been saying there was no good music in the 1980s, but after researching the timeline (see fig. 1, pages 13–15), I see I was wrong. It was *his* choices that were so awful!

Year	Grammy Award Record of the Year	Person of the Year	Inventions	In the News
2013	"Rolling in the Deep"	Pope Francis	Quantum computer	Obamacare
2012	"Somebody That I Used to Know"	Barack Obama	Cloud computing	Trayvon Martin
2011	"Need You Now"	The Protester	Stem cells from fat	Japan earthquake
2010	"Use Somebody"	Mark Zuckerberg	iPad	Haiti earthquake, BP oil spill
2009	"Please Read the Letter"	Ben Bernanke	Ares Rockets	Economic stimulus
2008	"Rehab"	Barack Obama	Retail DNA tests	Stock market decline
2007	"Not Ready to Make Nice"	Vladimir Putin	iPhone	Housing bubble bursts
2006	"Boulevard of Broken Dreams"	You	Induced stem cells, YouTube	Plot to blow up planes
2005	"Here We Go Again"	Bill & Melinda Gates, Bono	Twitter	Hurricane Katrina, Terri Schiavo
2004	"Clocks"	George W. Bush	SpaceShipOne	Tsunami
2003	"Don't Know Why"	The American Soldier	Toyota hybrid	Iraq war, gay marriage
2002	"Walk On"	The Whistleblowers	Blue Tooth	DC sniper
2001	"Beautiful Day"	Rudy Giuliani	iPod	9/11, Afghanistan
2000	"Smooth"	George W. Bush	Flash drive	Presidential election
1999	"My Heart Will Go On"	Jeff Bezos	DVR	Columbine
1998	"Sunny Came Home"	Bill Clinton, Ken Starr	Viagra	Clinton impeachment
1997	"Change the World"	Andy Grove	Nonmechanical MP3 player (iPod)	Death of Diana
1996	"Kiss from a Rose"	Dr. David Ho	USB	Bombing in Atlanta at the Summer Olympic Games

continued →

Year	Grammy Award Record of the Year	Person of the Year	Inventions	In the News
1995	"All I Wanna Do"	Newt Gingrich	JAVA, DVD	Oklahoma City bombing
1994	"I Will Always Love You"	Pope John Paul II	HIV Protease	Rwandan genocide
1993	"Tears in Heaven"	The Peacemakers	Smartphone, Pentium processor	Branch Davidians
1992	"Unforgettable"	Bill Clinton	Plasma color display	Rodney King
1991	"Another Day in Paradise"	Ted Turner	Webcam	Gulf War
1990	"Wind Beneath My Wings"	The Two George Bushes	World Wide Web	Mandela released
1989	"Don't Worry, Be Happy"	Mikhail Gorbachev	High-definition TV	Berlin wall comes down, Tiananmen Square
1988	"Graceland"	Endangered Earth	Digital cell phone	Michael Milken
1987	"Higher Love"	Mikhail Gorbachev	Statins, disposable contacts	Iran-Contra affair
1986	"We Are the World"	Corazon Aquino	MIR space station, disposable camera	Chernobyl, Challenger
1985	"What's Love Got to Do with It"	Deng Xiaoping	MS Windows	New Coke, Reagan-Gorbachev
1984	"Beat It"	Peter Ueberroth	Portable CD player, Apple Mac	Subway vigilante
1983	"Rosanna"	Ronald Reagan	PDA , Internet, Apple Lisa	Bombing of Beirut marine barracks
1982	"Bette Davis Eyes"	The computer	CD player, camcorder, artificial heart	Tylenol scare
1981	"Sailing"	Lech Walesa	Graphical User Interface, MS DOS	Charles and Diana marry

Year	Grammy Award Record of the Year	Person of the Year	Inventions	In the News
1980	"What a Fool Believes"	Ronald Reagan	Compact Disc	John Lennon shot
1979	"Just the Way You Are"	Ayatollah Khomeini	Walkman	Camp David peace treaty
1978	"Hotel California"	Teng Hsiao-P'ing	Spreadsheet, bottled water	Panama Canal returned
1977	"This Masquerade"	Anwar Sadat	Mobile phone, personal stereo	Death of Elvis
1976	"Love Will Keep Us Together"	Jimmy Carter	Ink jet printer	OPEC raises price of oil $13.30
1975	"I Honestly Love You"	American Women	digital camera, laser printer	US recession
1974	"Killing Me Softly"	King Faisal	Hybrid vehicle	Watergate
1973	"The First Time Ever I Saw Your Face"	John J. Sirica	Personal computer, email	US leaves Vietnam
1972	"It's Too Late"	Nixon & Kissinger	Ethernet	Equal Rights amendment
1971	"Bridge Over Troubled Water"	Richard Nixon	LCD, MRI, VCR microprocessor	US wage freeze
1970	"Aquarius"	Willy Brandt	Pocket calculator, relational database, floppy disc	Voting age reduced
1969	"Mrs. Robinson"	The Middle Americans	Bar code scanner	Woodstock
1968	"Up, Up and Away"	Astronauts Anders, Borman, Lovell	RAM	MLK assassination
1967	"Strangers in the Night"	Lyndon B. Johnson	Handheld calculator	Detroit riots
1966	"A Taste of Honey"	Twenty-five and under	Fuel injection	Cigarette warning labels
1965	"Girl from Ipanema"	Gen. Westmoreland	CD	Watts race riots

Sources: "Grammy Awards" 2012; "Headlines That Shaped History" 2007; "News and Events on This Day in History" 2012; "Public's Top Stories" 2010; "TIME's Person of the Year" 2012; "Timeline of United States Inventions (After 1991)" 2012; "Timeline of United States Inventions (1946–1991)" 2012; "The Top Story Index" 2012.

Figure 1: Generational timeline.

If values, experiences, and music do indeed define your generational cohort, it follows that when the world changes fast,
generations get shorter. For the timeline in figure
1, I went straight to the Internet. Music titles came
from rockonthenet.com; time.com sourced the historical list; and most of the inventions were on a list
from Wikipedia. Top news stories are from *USA
Today*, Pew Research, and the People History Blog.
Take a look at the timeline, and see if you can detect
enough commonalities to identify generations.

*A generation is
determined by
the values and
experiences of our
youth as anchored
by the music and
ceremony of
the times.*

We connect and we group, based on shared values and shared
experiences. That means that I, a sixty-four-year-old white
Protestant male, would more likely have common ground with
a fifty-five-year-old black Protestant female than I would with a
thirty-year-old white, single, New Age male. And, as noted previously, news travels fast. Looking at the timeline, what experience do Millennials in Egypt have in common with Millennials in
Tennessee? Technology. Digital technology.

But it's not just accepting technology, or even understanding
it, that separates the generations. It's *how* they use technology that
says it all. Take something as common as a cell phone. Boomers
(86.6 percent) and Millennials (86.7 percent) have nearly an identical rate of ownership, but they don't use them the same way. Tim
Miller, of Sitel, Inc., told me, "The difference between Gen X and
Y is obvious in our Cyber Cafe. Gen X people get on the computer
to check their email while Gen Y is looking at their phone." That
was true the day of the interview, but I am willing to bet it is no
longer a fact considering the rate at which Gen X and Boomers are
catching up to the more tech-savvy Millennials.

Notice in figure 2 that Gen X and Millennial percentages are
much higher in instant messaging and online communities than the
Boomer percentages. They are definitely leading the pack! Also
notice where the generations are similar. The sum of the percentage totals may be greater than 100 because the respondents can
select more than one answer.

After searching online, how do you communicate with others about a service, product, or brand? (Check all that apply)	Millennial	Gen X	Boomer	All
Blogging	15.5%	7.4%	2.3%	6.3%
Cell Phone	54.5%	42.0%	31.4%	36.8%
Email	44.6%	54.51%	54.8%	52.4%
Face-to-Face	62.9%	69.5%	68.0%	65.7%
Instant Messaging	37.7%	19.2%	8.4%	16.8%
Online Communities/Social Media (Facebook, Twitter, and so on)	38.1%	24.7%	11.2%	19.6%
Telephone (Landline)	21.9%	27.5%	37.1%	32.2%
Text Messaging	44.0%	31.7%	15.4%	24.3%
Other (please specify)	0.9%	1.2%	2.3%	2.2%

Source: BIGinsight™, Media Behaviors & Influence Study *(Worthington, OH: Prosper Business Development, 2011).*

Figure 2: How do you communicate?

Appreciate the Good News

Ask a Boomer to describe a Millennial, and you might wrongly hear, "No common sense, no work ethic, no clue." For all their faults (of course, we Boomers have none), Millennials have plenty to offer.

They are fast thinkers and multitaskers, and they can quickly separate out what is important to them. Though fiercely loyal to themselves, they adapt easily and thrive on change. Give them interesting work, recognition, and a chance to learn. Train them well (they hate looking stupid), and keep them informed. They are not about to wear a dumb-looking uniform, they eat when they're hungry and not by the clock, and they aren't likely to use a rigid sales patter—if they're willing to sell at all. This is the first truly techno-fearless generation, so stay out of their way. Oh, and they do just fine with diversity, which is a good thing because the world no longer looks the way it did in 1958—which is also a good thing.

What about the Traditionals? They value hard work, trust, formality, authority, institutional leadership, and social order, particularly if there are stories or history associated. Traditionals are private, tending to publicly withhold their emotions. While this generation was defined by letters sent via US mail (yes, in cursive!), most have transitioned to using email. Most master technology when they realize its potential. However, their preferred communication is a face-to-face visit.

Traditionals do not like waste. They do not waste food, money, or any other resource, including time—theirs or yours, a result of growing up during the great economic depression as well as experiencing rationing of food and fuel during World Wars I and II.

It is a myth that they have more accidents. What is true, according to the AARP, is that older workers have fewer on-the-job accidents.[1] Many Traditionals prefer to work rather than retire, which bears out the fact that people of all ages like meaningful work. Older workers are as productive as younger workers, and here is a fact to cheer some of us up: intelligence remains the same until we're in our late seventies!

And the Boomers? Like Gen X and the Millennials, they value competition that declares winners and losers. Boomers value hard work, success, teamwork, and for the most part are anti-rules and regulations. Their era saw a war in Vietnam that divided the nation and gave rise to the age of war protests, flower children, and the widespread use of illegal drugs. Boomers invented the term *workaholic*, and quite a few get their therapy riding a Harley. (If you see a Harley club riding by, be sure to wave at your CPA, family attorney, and district judge.) Should you ask a Boomer where he grew up, you are likely to hear, "Don't know. I haven't grown up yet!" The oldest Boomers are turning sixty-five, but don't count them out—their average life expectancy is just shy of seventy-nine.

Now for Gen X. While Boomers and Millennials have a well-defined persona, Gen X has difficulty being defined in the demographic landscape. Many Gen Xs think of themselves as younger Boomers or early Millennials. In many ways, Gen X could rightfully be called the Bridge Generation. It is as if Gen X is on hold, waiting for the Millennials to mature. (I love a statement Lady Gaga made on *The Ellen DeGeneres Show*: "Every night I feel invigorated by the crowd. I've been working so hard all my life to be too busy to sleep. I am so excited to be tired!" I believe her statement says, as an early Millennial, "I finally matter!")

Their contributions to music, fashion, and even political movements seem to be overshadowed by the earlier 1960s rock, peace marches, civil rights progress, and the development of fast food (as if that were cause for pride!), all pioneered by the omnipresent Boomers. In fact, though Gen Xs seem to live in the shadow of the Boomers, they are more than just junior Boomers. They have a culture of their own. The National Oceanographic and Atmospheric Administration's Office of Diversity suggests that Gen X be recognized for an entrepreneurial spirit, valued not for being very loyal, but for their independent and creative thinking.

Gen X traits include the following:

- Need continuous feedback, although not as much as Millennials

- Value work/life balance

- Prefer to communicate via email and want you to do the same

- Talk in short sound bites and give lots of informal feedback

- Do not want to live in the Boomer shadow; they want to be asked their opinion

So what do we do? Offer Traditional-class, Boomer-class, Gen X-class, and Millennial-class service?

As a matter of fact, that is exactly what you must do. Even though the gap is closing quickly, each generation is different and demands a slightly different approach in customer service. But as we have said before, the differences are usually more a matter of context than content.

Don't Bucket

Every time I sit at my keyboard and think about the Millennials, a
little voice in my head whispers, "Don't bucket! Don't bucket!" That
little voice is reminding me not to put every Millennial into the same
bucket.

The Millennial you *think* you know is well educated, highly
social, and a multitasker. There are other Millennials who you
probably don't know. They are not all the squeaky-clean college
types from nice neighborhoods in the American suburbs. They might
live in the American ghetto or in poverty on the other side of the
world. Throw in any other descriptors, real or imagined, and you are
still wrong . . . because Millennials come in a broad rainbow of
color, language, and social settings. Yet they *are* still Millennials
because they all have one thing in common: they have all grown up
in an age when digital information is powerful. (Think Tunisia,
Egypt, Libya, and Occupy Wall Street.)

If you intend to label this diverse generation, you are going to
have to do better than personality traits. Stick to values, experiences, and music, and you will not be far off the mark.

A cohort shares the experiences of its times, and
those experiences shape its values. To restate this,
the behavior of the cohort will reflect the experiences and values its members share, but membership in a cohort is not determined by behavior. It's

*A cohort is
determined by
shared values, not
shared behaviors.*

also not determined solely by age. If you doubt that, I invite you
to go shopping with my mother the next time she needs new tires.

If you take away a single message, let it be that understanding your customer is the foundation to serving your customer. If
you have space for one additional concept, let it be that there is no
hard-and-fast rule for determining an individual's membership in
a demographic cohort. In the end, we are all different, and different is good!

CHAPTER 2

Portrait of a Millennial

H ere we sit, about to be hit by a tidal wave of consumers who have a slightly different take on how to relate to a company, its products, its people, and its other customers. At the same time, the larger market, aided and abetted by the Millennials, is becoming increasingly more demanding.

Not many years ago, customers were essentially offered a choice: service, quality, price—you could have two. A print shop in our neighborhood used to have this cartoon on the wall. Over the drawing of a person rolling on the floor laughing was this saying: "You want it fast? You want it good? You want it cheap? Pick any two, and call me tomorrow."

Today's customers won't settle for two. They want all three. Every generation—Millennials, Gen X, Boomers, even the Traditionals—wants it all. Service. Quality. Price. Why? Because the baby bears have taught mama and papa bear the new tricks of the Internet; the Millennial mindset is not limited to folks of a certain age.

What do you do? You listen to your customers! Make it your business to learn how they think so you can position yourself in a way that attracts their attention and keeps their loyalty. That's what this chapter is about: understanding who they are and how they view the world.

My Way, Right Away, Why Pay?

If a generation had a mantra, "my way, right away, why pay?" would fit Millennials perfectly. It is also, let me point out, a bare-bones strategy for anyone who wants to attract today's consumer.

The Millennials believe that all things are possible. They want the world their way, and they want it now. They have grown up in a text-it or FedEx-it, why-wait world, and they don't expect to wait. They *expect* unlimited choices, and they would like you to customize your product just for them. And did I mention that they see no need to pay for the additional work their request might entail? As far as they are concerned, *you should be paying them* for helping you improve your product.

They take technology for granted. They live through social media. In fact, their customer service expectations have been shaped by the speed of technology and social media. They do their homework ahead of time, researching your product and competitive offers online. They are fast learners in negotiating. They negotiate *everything*. On the other hand, they will pay for service, but you must be prepared to earn your fee. What they expect from you in terms of service is very different from what you're used to delivering. Let's look at each of these characteristics in turn.

Technology Rules

Millennials grew up digital. They are not intimidated by technology, and they show little patience with those who shy away from using it to its full advantage. They expect to use technology to make work and life more interesting and productive, surfing the web wirelessly via smartphone or iPad. In fact, to a Millennial, failing to use technology to its fullest is almost as bad as not using it at all.

To reach Millennials, your website must look and feel personal and direct, with features that wow visitors with what feels like an in-person presentation. A lame website will not only fail to impress your Millennial customers, it will also be a point of embarrassment to your Millennial employees. They expect technology to be part of their work world outside of your website, too. Having the latest, even cutting-edge technology goes a long way in retaining a Millennial workforce. Let them get hands-on with the technology, and stand by to learn a thing or two.

Your website also has to stand up to the competition in terms of what you're offering, because Millennials live their lives online. They consider it both easy and sensible to research products they're considering. Know who your competition is, especially the online competition they'll be comparing you to, especially if you are a traditional retailer. If there are important differences in your favor, point them out to customers. Don't let low price be the deciding factor in the purchase decision. If you can't indicate any points of difference, you may turn your product or service into a commodity, and then price becomes the only factor in the Millennial's purchase decision.

How important is technology to Millennials? So important that they're willing to use guerilla tactics to train Boomers in how to use it.

I saw this in action while attending the annual meeting of the National Speakers Association (NSA), the association of choice for speaking professionals such as Zig Ziglar, Tony Robbins, and internet gurus Randy Gage and Ford Saeks. Hoping for a short respite from the crowd, I ducked into an unmarked meeting room and found myself right in the middle of a Millennial strategy session. I settled quietly into a chair at the back of the room but knew in an instant that I had been busted. A Millennial woman quickly moved to the empty chair beside me and whispered, "Sir!" (You know you're old when a Millennial calls you sir.) "Sir, you must be looking for the luncheon."

I feigned confusion and weakly asked, "Would it be all right with you if I sat here long enough to catch my breath and rest my aching feet?" (I am a pro when it comes to looking pitiful.)

In short order it became clear that the Millennials were plotting to take over the NSA; they were creating a formal plan. Their plot included a maneuver one might call "giving back first"; they decided to reverse-mentor the more experienced members, by pairing with an old timer and showing him or her how to use social marketing and a few other tricks for making the most of the latest technology.

At the end of the session, they declared a Tweet Up to be held at a nearby hotel. The host promised "enough power strips for everyone to recharge your devices."

Sheeesh. In my day, the host just provided ice for the beer!

Millennials have sometimes been ripped for being unprofessional and for having a sense of entitlement. Maybe there is some truth to that, but that's not been my experience.

Now if I could just get them to stop calling me sir.

Social Media Matters

Millennials are often credited with pioneering social media, and no doubt, as a group they are the power users of social media. But that doesn't matter, because Gen X and the Boomers are catching up. Social media is often hyped as the be-all and end-all of marketing. It isn't and it won't be, but ignore it at your peril. The mighty Bank of America has a Senior VP of Social Media. . . . Now tell me they don't think social media counts! Smart companies have already decided that social media has a promising potential as a place where you can talk to customers, listen to their feedback, and be there when they need help or have other concerns.

Social media is cool. But cool doesn't count unless it puts black ink on the bottom line. Fail to deliver on your service promise, and coolness won't count.

Social media is now key to efficiently delivering great customer service. It has become the technology of choice for most large companies. Be careful! If your only use of social media is to keep the cost of after-the-sale customer service as low as possible, you may be missing an even bigger opportunity. Social media could be described as a virtual meeting space where you can hang out with your customers. Your virtual address should be a place where customers can come to play, learn, and share . . . when *they* want to.

Millennials live online—or, more accurately, on text. Texting seems to be the preferred method of communication.

One evening when our kids had walked the six doors down our street to join us for dinner, the after-dinner conversation got suddenly quiet. Our grandson sat curled in a chair with his cell phone held in the familiar two-thumbed position. Not ten feet away, her feet tucked under her, was my granddaughter. She too was in the send mode. "You guys are awfully quiet," I said. "Who are you texting?"

Can you guess? They were texting each other!

Timing Is Everything

Millennials have grown up in a world of instants—instant messaging, instant delivery, instant everything. They want what they want when they want it, and see no reason to wait for anything. Labeling Millennials "impatient" may not be completely accurate or completely fair. When you live in a world where you can download a book in seconds, make arrangements for a cross-country business trip in a matter of minutes, and fly from a winter-cold Midwest to a tropical island in a few hours, maybe you're not being impatient at all!

If you are selling to Millennials:

- Rethink your product and service delivery systems, and eliminate as much of the wait time as possible.

- Do whatever it takes to make the wait an interesting, engaging part of the experience. Consider using wait time to train the customer how to use the product.

- Unbundle product delivery and waiting by offering premium delivery options.

We'll look more closely at unbundling a little later in this chapter.

Outstanding is good. Standing out is better.

Everything Is Negotiable

Millennials are whizzes at negotiating, and as you learned earlier in this chapter, they come prepared with thorough research. We don't know where they learned the art of negotiation, but they seem willing to negotiate almost anything. They know that products rarely stand alone. They know that products come with warranties, delivery, and sometimes training—all negotiable, from the Millennial perspective. They know that the cost of a help desk is buried somewhere in the price. They know that some things are unbundled and some are not, and they look to customize even when you haven't offered customization. And they know plenty about manipulating the system for freebies and other concessions.

Here's something interesting I heard in a recent focus group:

- "I bargain everywhere. I go to customer service and ask for at least 10 percent off."

- "I love it when they screw up. I'm always getting free stuff! I never leave unhappy."

These comments illustrate the "my way, right away, why pay?" Millennial mantra perfectly. And notice in your everyday transactions how Gen X, Boomers, and Traditionals are learning from the Millennials; soon all of your customers will expect the Millennial treatment. Read on, and we'll show you how to make the shift on your terms!

Sales Expectations Are Soaring

So now you know: Millennials arrive at your place of business, whether online or brick and mortar, having done lots of homework. They know their stuff, and they expect your sales team to know it, too. If they have technical questions, they expect competent, well-informed answers. If they want extra service, they expect you to make it happen.

But if they don't need help, they want your salespeople to disappear into the woodwork. Don't hover, don't bug—*be invisible*. Once their questions are asked, our job, as they see it, is to answer the questions quickly and accurately and then just leave.

By the way, our focus groups and surveys reveal that *all generations* feel that way. Gen X, Boomers, and Traditionals all agree: they want contact but don't want you to hover. They echo the

Millennials' refrain, "Be invisible" . . . until *they* decide they need you.

Our traditional idea of a salesperson doesn't work with Millennials. The ability to research a product at anytime from anywhere makes the idea of a salesperson as a walking source of information about features and benefits almost intrusive. What about the other, usually hidden, goal of a salesperson—to create a need? Well, Millennials don't appreciate being talked into a purchase.

So what should you do? First, the job of salesperson isn't going to disappear in the next ten minutes, so it's still important to train your sales staff in product knowledge. If you don't, chances are, your well-informed customers will question your price even more. Second, think about the logical and probable evolution of the salesperson. I believe salespersons will rapidly evolve to become sales *assistants*. They will demonstrate the product, make add-on suggestions, and generally facilitate the sale to customers who are ready and able to buy when they walk through your door, whether the door is real or virtual. Help your sales staff understand their changing roles.

"No matter what the product, you must have the ability to demonstrate your product. Because once the client takes mental possession of the product, our work is done. It is called the Soft Puppy close. Think about how hard it is to hand back a soft puppy after you have cuddled with it for a while. When you demo your product, do everything possible to make the experience feel like you are holding a soft puppy."
—Fred Vang

Millennials are causing customer service expectations to rise marketwide. Two significant trends are unfolding as I write. The first is that service is being unbundled and sold as an adjunct to the purchased product. Millennials are willing to pay extra for service as long as they see it as a good value. They are big on "deliverables." The second is that both the product and the accompanying service are being personalized and customized. We have to understand both trends from the Millennial perspective and their allegiance to social media.

Unbundled Service

Our research indicates that digital consumers (and remember, all generations are now digital consumers) are smart consumers—smart enough to recognize the value of information or privilege, and willing to pay for it . . . *if* they are made aware of it. For example, a theme park's unbundled service product might be VIP passes that allow you to go to the head of the line—an idea now in play at the Disney and Universal theme parks.

> *The elements most likely to be unbundled, because of demand, are information and customer service.*

The elements most likely to be unbundled, because of demand, are information and customer service, such as product training for an exclusive cookware set or preboarding privileges for premium airline customers.

Service Good Enough to Sell

During the 2011 holiday season, a whopping 25.3 percent of holiday shoppers admit they shopped the brick-and-mortar stores but purchased online. Of that group, 74.9 percent reported that price was the big motivator, followed closely by convenience.[2]

One thing I didn't see in the blog was a demographic description of the "Price Check" shoppers, but I'm willing to bet the demographics skew toward a younger, mostly Millennial group. Why? Because Millennials as a group tend to be better-informed consumers who don't hesitate to negotiate.

My way, right away, why pay? That's the Millennial mantra. Millennials have grown up in a world that has left them with high expectations. They see no reason why they can't have things the way they want them, when they want them, and they can't see much reason why you should profit from doing business with them. Millennial shoppers do their homework. They know about the product, the price, and promotions. They are ready and willing to deal.

What does this mean to retailers? Whether you are a traditional Main Street retailer or a high-tech online provider, you have to ask yourself one question: Is my customer service good enough to sell? If it isn't, why would you expect a Millennial shopper who has done his homework to hesitate to fire up the smartphone and make the best deal possible?

Information That Adds Value

Many products have an information or knowledge component: consider the television that guides the purchaser through the set-up procedure, or the cell phone that can provide turn-by-turn directions to the nearest bagel shop. Keep in mind that if the customer is not aware of those features, adding them to the product adds to the *cost* but does not contribute to the *value*. Also keep in mind that great customer service, if marketed properly, can keep look-alike products from becoming commodities.

For example, the popular hamburger chain Five Guys has unit sales often many times of the competition—but their product offering isn't substantially different from their look-alike competitors. What's the difference? At Five Guys, you can read a whiteboard message informing you that the potatoes used in today's batch of French fries come from Farmer Smith's Potato Farm in Idaho. All of a sudden you have two products that in a blind taste test would probably be indistinguishable. But who wouldn't prefer a home-grown Farmer Smith potato over a generic potato that comes in a box? Sharp marketing creates a point of difference that adds value.

Customized Product and Service

The second trend is called *mass customization*, and it simply means that, thanks to computer-assisted manufacturing, for many products, customization is not a big deal. The efficiencies you used to receive from long production runs aren't the big deal they used to be, either. In the past, stamping out identical items without having to constantly reset or reconfigure the production line kept costs down. Today, with computer-assisted production, setting up for a slightly different product can be done almost instantly.

Custom fit, custom trimmed, custom tuned . . . if you type really fast, sometimes you'll find *customized* comes out *customer*. Maybe that's the lesson: give the product or service to the customer exactly the way she wants it. Pillow too soft? Salsa too mild? Bangs a bit too long? Customers don't have to accommodate our offerings anymore. Instead, we accommodate their needs.

Whatever their rationale, today's Millennial consumers want things their way. Call it selfish, call it stupid, but if you're smart, you'll figure out how to make your product or service any way the customer wants. One hundred years ago, it might have worked for Henry Ford to deliver his assembly-line cars in any color the customer wanted, so long as it was black. Today, ignore customization at your peril!

What should you do? You can take the old-fashioned, all-or-nothing approach, or you can get with the program and sell your customer service options and customization as accessories.

Customers expect products that are customized for them. Customers now expect service that is customized, too.

Consider this example. Recently a new frozen yogurt concept opened near our home. Customers pick up an empty, squat paper cup and then dispense an assortment of delicious frozen yogurt in flavors and quantities of their choosing. Then they wander along a stainless steel counter and pick from a large selection of toppings. At the end, their goodies are weighed, and a smiling clerk announces the price . . . a perfect example of customized product and unbundled service!

Honda Gets Lucky

If you live on the west coast, you may have noticed the increasing popularity of Honda among the young people. So far nothing coming from Detroit has caught their attention like the Honda line. Honda, being smart marketers asked their top market what else they would like to buy.

According to their research the younger set said they would love the Honda Element, a boxy, terminally ugly mini-van with a wide-open, hose-it-down interior. Oh, yeh? Well, they stayed away in droves! Instead, Honda got lucky when the middle-aged crowd went for the Element in a big way!

Millennial Rule: Your customers don't always know what they want.

('Betcha you didn't predict so many people would buy a Snuggie!)

Millennials at Work

By now you may be wondering who's delivering all this great customized unbundled service. Well, people like to buy from people like themselves. So if you're planning to build a sales team of Millennials, (1) good for you, and (2) you'll need to understand how they feel about work.

If you automatically complete the sentence "Freedom's just another word . . ." without thinking, I can be pretty sure you're not a Millennial. And if you can hum a melody to the lyric "Let me entertain you," you probably aren't even a Gen X. In either case you have a problem, because any anthem for Millennials has to pay tribute to the gods of Millennials—the god of freedom and the god of entertainment.

Millennials are replacing control with freedom and empowerment. While that may manifest itself today, to some, as being spoiled and coddled, I'm betting this freedom will morph into a sense of responsibility. I'm also betting that a generation that grew up being constantly entertained will continue to require constant stimulation. They tend to bring entertainment and fun into the workplace, as well as creativity and innovation.

Birds of a Feather

Here's something to think about: Millennials flock. As an employer, that's good. Catch one, and you may catch a bunch. But be careful—lose one, and he will take his peeps with him.

They embrace this truth: work should be fun. For them, the line between work and leisure begins to blur. One possible result could be *more* productivity, not less. And this value may account for their attachment to being on a team, staying with their friends.

Millennials expect work to be rewarding, and only those companies that provide meaningful, attainable paths for growth are likely to earn their loyalty as employees. Three stellar examples of fun but responsible workplaces are Rack Space, Zappos, and my favorite, Southwest Airlines.

When Southwest decided to take on the lucrative California commuter routes, they came under heavy fire from United Airlines, among others. Not willing to see their beloved airline come in second, Southwest employees spent their own money and used their own travel passes, on their own time, to serve as unpaid reinforcements in the battle for California customers. Fly SWA, and if you pay attention, you will often see off-duty SWA flight attendants working with the regular crew to expedite drink service when onboard as passengers.

And they still find time for fun. Southwest Airlines is famous for doing intuitively what Buns and I learned to do on purpose.

Flying from Memphis to Houston, a flight attendant recognized me and said, "Aren't you that positively outrageous guy?"

"As a matter of fact, I am," I replied, pleased to be recognized.

"Would you happen to have one of your books that I could give away to one of our customers?"

"Sure!"

I didn't know what would happen. I just knew it would be fun. At thirty thousand feet, the intercom rang out, "Ladies and gentlemen. We're fortunate today to have Southwest Airlines' author in residence, T. Scott Gross, on board. If you would like to win a copy of his book *Positively Outrageous Service*, use the napkin that we are handing out to guess the number of sheets of toilet paper it takes to stretch from the aft lav to the forward lav."

Then, much to the amusement of the customers, a flight attendant came racing down the aisle unfurling a roll of TP as she went! (The answer is 172, just in case this ever happens to you!)

SWA has hundreds of Millennials who know that when they are having fun, you are having fun, too. What a great place to work!

Millennials are fun, smart, and easy to find . . . just look in the basement, according to urban legend. One night a full-fledged Millennial was teaching me (on YouTube) how to create video graphics when an intercom went off and a woman's voice with a Brooklyn accent said, "Bryan? Can you come up here for a minute?"

"Ma! I'm on the computer. I can't come up right now!" Then he turned back to the camera, sighed, and said, "It's my mom. Sheeesh!"

I rest my case!

Millennials at Home

As I've been studying the Millennials, I've learned some interesting details about their lifestyles. I'll let you decide whether the following observations can be turned into an advantage for your business.

First, it may be economics or it could easily be something in the water, but Millennials are in no hurry to leave home, marry, raise a family, or mow the lawn. One in three (38 percent) still live with parents.

A survey by TwentySomething.com and reported in Money.CNN .com puts the percentage of college graduates who will return home at a whopping 85 percent![3] Maybe it's because, according to a study by Rutgers University, nearly 30 percent of college graduates will fail to land a job within six months, and those who do will be paid less than their predecessors.[4] Whatever the reason, the Boomer generation sees Millennials as being lazy. Maybe they are. Certainly they're late in leaving the security of home.

Millennials are also in no hurry to give up their nights and weekends with their buds. According to US census data, nearly half of women between twenty-five and twenty-nine have never married.[5] As recently as 1986, that number was only one-fourth! In 1950, the average age for marriage was twenty-three for men, twenty for women. Today, many Millennials don't view marriage as important as the earlier generations did, and when they do, they marry later—age twenty-eight for men, twenty-six for women.

Second, like the rest of us, Millennials have learned to be financially responsible. In fact, if you look closely at figure 3 (page 30), you will see that they are more responsible than all generations combined. More pay the entire credit card balance each month, and fewer have a card at all.

Regarding your credit card debt, do you ...	Millennials	All
Pay the balance in full each month	46.8%	35.1%
Pay a portion of the balance	33.5%	28.6%
Pay the minimum	7.8%	10.4%
I don't have a credit cards	11.9%	25.9%

Source: BIGinsight™, Media Behaviors & Influence Study *(Worthington, OH: Prosper Business Development, 2011).*

Figure 3: Credit card debt.

Third, Millennials spend a lot of time online, a lot of time watching TV (often online), and a lot of time tweeting (see fig. 4). How do they find the time? Simple—they are media multitaskers.

Which of the following online activities do you regularly do for fun and entertainment?	Millennial	Gen X	Boomer
Play video games	49.6%	27.0%	16.4%
IM/Chat	44.7%	31.3%	10.2%
Download music/video	43.7%	32.6%	16.5%
Shop online	38.9%	44.4%	41.5%
Use Facebook and other social media	37.1%	34.9%	23.4%
Watch TV shows online	37.5%	25.9%	18.3%

Source: BIGinsight™, Media Behaviors & Influence Study *(Worthington, OH: Prosper Business Development, 2011).*

Figure 4: Online activities for fun.

It's a given that Millennials use multiple sources of social media at the same time. If they do it on their time, no problem. If they do it on your time, on the job, you might consider redirecting that multitasking mindset to more challenging work.

In fact, you can take advantage of their desire to multitask by cross-training Millennials in multiple skill areas. They'll love it, and you'll wind up with more valuable employees. Fire/EMS services are terrific examples of the effectiveness of cross-training.

Make cross-training a feature of your career path, and watch how people clamor to learn more!

The focus group was mostly Gen X business professionals. It cracked me up to hear a Gen X real estate developer describe his feelings about Millennials by saying, "Sometimes I want to open the window and yell at them to keep off the lawn!" He acknowledged that the differences between generations aren't often a matter of good or bad. Sometimes our differences are just . . . different.

I asked the group about tattoos, and I admit I was appalled to discover that participants averaged about two tats each. I wanted to yell, "Hey, dummy! They don't come off!" And then I remembered: our differences are not always a matter of good different or bad different. They are simply a matter of being different.

A Millennial Snapshot (source: Pew Research)

- 70% have a tattoo hidden by clothes
- 40% of Millennials have two tattoos
- 18% have six or more tattoos

Action Steps

If you are dealing with Millennials or a Millennial mindset, do this.

Think of a paycheck as a product that people purchase in exchange for their time, talent, and effort. When looked at in that light, *every* transaction could be considered as a sale. Here's the point: if you want your customers to be loyal and to pay top dollar for doing business with you, then the to-do list that follows applies equally to your employees . . . who are, in a sense, purchasing their paycheck!

- **Customize**—They want it their way. Customize your service as well as your product.

- **Personalize**—It builds loyalty to the product.

- **Socialize**—It builds loyalty to other customers.

- **Organize**—Millennials are natural-born team players. Put everyone on a team, even your customers! (Customers will give you feedback that you will get nowhere else . . . and even build your product for you. The open source Linux is a prime example, as are Wikipedia and the customer forums run by Intuit.)

- **Tangibilize**—If you do something that adds value, tell your customers.

- **Deflect and intercept**—Be where they are, when they are there, with the help they need.

- **Listen**—Customers won't share the important things until they believe you are listening.

Don't do this:

- Don't approach Millennial customers with a canned sales patter. They don't like to be treated like a number.

- Don't worry about engaging them with non-native speakers. They value diversity as long as it comes with competence.

- Don't worry about making them wait. Worry instead about making the wait worth it. In spite of their "my way, right away, why pay?" mantra, Millennials will happily wait—if, and only if, the wait adds value to the experience. Make the wait part of the service. Make it an interesting and valuable use of their time.

Think about the Olive Garden. While you were waiting, they plugged your pie hole with hot, chewy garlic breadsticks. And admit it, the previews are part of the reason you like to go to the movies. It isn't important how long customers wait. What counts is how they *feel* about the wait.

That's the Millennial list. Do you see anything there that wouldn't apply equally to all of your customers?

Your New Customer

So who is the new customer? For the moment, it is the Millennial. (Gen X has been around too long to be called new.) And instead of asking who our new customer is, we might ask, "Who is the latest *influence*?" That title appropriately belongs to the Millennials, but only for the moment. With Boomers catching up with technology, they have come closer to matching Millennials' buying habits.

So let's look at Millennials and note how their collective personality is impacting the delivery of customer service. Millennials have the following characteristics:

- **They are collaborative shoppers**—Millennials are team players; they even apply it to shopping! When shopping, they text their friends for real-time input on purchasing decisions.

- **They are time sensitive**—I started to write that Millennials don't like to waste their time, but they waste (in my opinion) plenty of time. What they don't like is for *you* to waste their time.

  Think about it. How do Millennials like to communicate? It seems as though their lives are lived 140 characters at a time on Twitter. Is that shallow, or is it simply a more effective use of time? Come to think about it, if you can't say it in 140 characters, maybe you aren't being clear, maybe the message is too big, or maybe you *are* wasting time.

- **They prefer social media for contact**—Try to arrange a sit-down, face-to-face meeting with a Millennial and what do you get? "Why?" or "Let's just Skype." And those messages are not likely to be delivered via voice. No, they are emailed or, more than likely, texted.

  In fact, Melinda Marcus, inPSYCHS Consultive Coach and Speaker, role-plays interview situations and presentation scenarios with job-seeking Gen Xs and Millennials because they tend to find face-to-face interviews difficult.

- **They are willing to pay**—"FedEx it" is heard all over the corporate world, to the point that *FedEx* is considered a verb even when the carrier is not FedEx. Ask yourself, if you worked in a FedEx-it environment with the I-want-it-now mindset, how patient would you be about waiting at the doctor's office? The research we conducted for *The Service Prescription* revealed that people aged eighteen through thirty-four would pay, on average, $26.45 to get better service at a doctor's office. A Boomer, aged forty-seven through sixty-five, would be far mellower. They would pony up a measly $7.84! I interpret that statistic to mean Millennials are willing to pay for great service.

  Unfortunately, our surveys also reveal that the average consumer, not only Millennials, believes that the cost of great customer service is built into the price.

  Here are two key points. First, while Boomers are likely to endure poor service and simply not return, Millennials are likely to demand compensation—as well as tell all their Facebook friends about the bad experience. Second, if you do something for a customer that would add value if the customer knew about it, then for goodness sake, tell the customer you are doing it!

(I know. I have mentioned this before, but it's worth repeating!) You have to help the customer reach the conclusion that no matter the price of your product, it's a price that represents a value, and the product is worth it.

We do have to be careful here, though. On one hand, it appears that the new consumer (Millennials) will pay a premium for great customer service; on the other hand, even though they may be willing to pay for great service, too often good service isn't part of the offering.

Here are the facts. In a study by CBS News, 64 percent of those polled said they had left a store because of poor service, and 67 percent reported hanging up on a service line without getting a solution.[6] We are surprised this next number isn't even larger—a whopping 71 percent said they were tremendously annoyed if they could not reach a real person on the phone.

- **They have disposable income**—Yes, they have an unemployment rate nearly three times the national average, and yes, just shy of two million Millennials have given up even attempting to find work, and yes, again, Millennials account for roughly 40 percent of US unemployed. BUT . . . hidden in this avalanche of disappointment, more than twenty million Millennials live at home. (Be careful . . . college students who live in dorms are counted as living at home!) Wait, there's more! As you would expect, as Millennials age the number of young people living with their parents declines considerably.[7]

When all the adjustments for age and college living arrangements are considered, Millennials, as a cohort, have money to burn mainly because so many are living at home. Dollars that otherwise would have gone to housing expenses are free to go anywhere the Millennial heart desires!

What is your household status?	Millennials	Gen X	Boomers	All 18+
Own	27.4%	59.7%	77.4%	63.6%
Rent	40.9%	33.8%	20.4%	27.1%
Live with parents or family	31.8%	6.5%	2.2%	9.2%

Source: BIGinsight™, Media Behaviors & Influence Study *(Worthington, OH: Prosper Business Development, 2011).*

Figure 5: Home ownership.

- **They want to be trained**—Millennials tell us that job training is important to them. During high unemployment especially, any job they take may not match their expertise from college, so they will need training. This creates two dilemmas: (1) they tend not to stay long enough for their employer to recoup its training dollars; and (2) they want to learn and are ready to learn, but they don't want to waste time learning anything not immediately useful to them. This forces companies to rethink their methods of training. Businesses need to train efficiently, by using materials that deliver the specific training the learner needs when the learner needs it. Not only is this *just-in-time* or *matrix* training the way Millennials want to be trained, it's also more effective than traditional training. In the traditional setting, training is delivered in classrooms with students of varying ability, and often it's delivered so far in advance of its on-the-job application that students have little or no retention. Matrix training, on the other hand, is likely to be delivered one student at a time and perhaps only minutes before the student puts the knowledge to use.

  This same line of thinking has direct carryover to training your customers. (Yes, you read that right. You *can* train your customers.) If you are selling a product that has a learning curve, the materials created for customer training should be arranged so that customers of different levels of expertise can learn what they need from the product just when they need to know it, without needing to wade through instructions that don't apply at that moment. (Why do we see so many versions of the For-Dummies books? I rest my case.)

Nobody gets excited about a job where they lack the skills and training to be successful. There is no more important day than the first day. Fred Vang says, "If you are going to teach a kid to fish, make certain they catch at least something the first time out."

Before we move on, take another look at the Millennial-pleasing ideas presented in this chapter. Notice, please, that with a few exceptions, these ideas can be implemented easily, inexpensively, and immediately. You can do it your way, right away—and no need to pay!

Now turn the page. You are about to become *invisible*!

It's impossible to avoid training because employees are learning something whether you like it or not!

PART TWO
The Message From Millennials

CHAPTER 3

"Don't *Sell* Me Anything"

Your new customers want you to stop selling. And that's what I want, too. I want you to toss aside what you think you know about sales tricks and fancy closes and instead adopt a mindset that says, "We're going to give up selling. We don't sell. We *serve*." Successful selling in that mindset means matching your product and your price to your customer. When you do that, there is no need for a tricky close.

Of course that holds true for all your customers, but it's especially true for Millennials. They have a unique take on what the customer-seller relationship should be.

> "If you have a good product and a qualified customer, all you have to do is put them together and . . . it is magic!" —Fred Vang

Become Invisible

That's right; your customers want you to disappear.

When Customers Talk was based on interviews of nearly ten thousand consumers polled online by BIGinsight of Dublin, Ohio, every month for two years—from 2002 to 2004. Counting all the questions we asked each month, we received more than twelve million individual data points. (You can't ignore numbers like that!) *Cluster technology*, a form of artificial intelligence, was used to analyze the verbatim responses.

So what did our panelists—your customers—say was the most important element of a service transaction? Sales and service staff who are knowledgeable and available. But that's not all. They also said that when they don't need a salesperson, they don't even want to see one. It is almost as if customers have two minds. One is crying, "Help me! I need you!" while the other, the evil twin Skippy, is saying, "Get out of the house!"

On one hand, you are supposed to be instantly available; on the other hand, they would really like it if you could become invisible until they need you. Just disappear.

Not many people like to be sold. They like to shop, they like to buy, but when the decisions are their own, they like not feeling manipulated. "I picked this out myself" feels so much better than leaving the store thinking the salesperson was the only one who got anything out of the transaction. So how can sales transactions satisfy the customer while being barely noticed or invisible?

A commitment to selling invisibly begins with a commitment to a set of values that puts the customer first. Over the last twenty years, as an author, speaker, and businessman who has owned multiple businesses with ten to thirty employees, I practiced these values religiously:

- If you want a business to last, put the customers first.
- Your passion should be evident in the product.
- Smart solutions beat big solutions.

And then there are the Ten Truisms of Selling Invisibly.

1. Everyone *can* sell, but not everyone *should* sell.

2. We all sell all the time, whether we are selling product, service, ideas, or relationships.

3. The better you know the customer, the more likely your pitch will be a perfect pitch.

4. There is a perfect pitch for every buyer/seller combination.

5. There is not one perfect pitch.

6. A perfect pitch is the pitch most likely to get you closer to a yes.

7. A perfect pitch ethically creates a tension to buy.

8. A perfect pitch does more than culminate in a sale; it benefits both buyer and seller.

9. The fundamental measure of a pitch is repeat and referral business.

10. The best pitch does not look like a pitch at all. The best pitch is invisible!

Now here's some good news. Invisible selling isn't new stuff. It is old stuff put in the right order!

Let me tell you a story. I call it "Fred the Inventor."

Fred Vang invented invisible selling. He didn't call it invisible selling, but that's what it was. In fact, Fred did not intentionally invent anything. He just needed a job.

But Fred is, if there is such a thing, a natural salesperson. No, that's not right. Fred doesn't *sell* anything. He just does what he does (and does it well, I should add), and the customers buy. And buy. And buy some more. If Fred is selling, you surely cannot see it. So he must use invisible selling.

Fred was a college student who needed a job if he intended to eat. So he pointed his used VW toward the nearest VW dealership and asked for a job.

"Fred," said the dealer, "I'm just not going to hire you. You look too young to know cars, and you would be sharing your time with college. When you finish, you'll be gone. I don't think our customers will buy from someone your age."

"That may be a good reason not to hire me," Fred said, "but there are a few good reasons in my favor that you should consider." The dealer nodded as if to say, "Go on."

"First, I know the product inside and out. I would be willing to bet I know as much about VW as any one of your salespeople. Second, I know everyone on campus, they trust me, and I love recommending VW. That will turn into sales. By the way, how many cars would you expect me to sell in a month?"

"If you can sell five, you would be doing very well."

"Then let me start today, and if, by the end of the month, I have sold six or more, then you keep me. If not, I'll leave on my own, and you will owe me nothing."

"Son, you have got yourself a deal!"

That first month, Fred sold sixteen new and used automobiles!

Reminiscing about that experience, Fred told me, "They had me share an office with a truly grotesque human being, who would snort, spit, and continuously clear his throat. We called him Rhino. He would go to the drinking fountain, wrap his fat lips completely around the fixture, and suck the water out of the fountain.

"There was a beautiful Westfalia pop-top camper on the show-room floor near the door, so I asked the boss if I could set up an office in the van; anything to get away from Rhino, the living Petri dish. The boss okayed it but thought I was out of my mind. I guess he figured I would be gone in a matter of weeks and there was no point in arguing.

"On Fridays, I would call my Saturday appointments and advise them not to eat breakfast. Saturday I would get to work early, push the van out of the showroom, and when my customers arrived, I would say, 'We're having pancakes and eggs. How would you like your eggs?'

"We didn't talk cars; we didn't talk features and benefits. We would just eat and look at maps and talk about the places they would go on their first trip. And then they would ask to buy the camper."

That's the way Fred does it. For him, invisible selling comes naturally. The rest of us have to work at it. Stand by to learn how it's done!

"The best salespeople see things through their customer's eyes, modify their styles to their customer's chemistry, and pull together their offering to meet their customer's needs. But being in front of the customer doesn't help if you do all the talking." —Beth Klein, President/CEO, GE Medical Systems

---

Light the Sales FUSE

Let's look at a sales process that is flexible enough to be appropriate for any selling situation. However, keep in mind that the digital generation hates sales scripts as much as they love having things their way. That is a gentle hint to remind you that even though I am about to give you a formula, I have no intention of even implying that you should use it 100 percent of the time.

When you think selling, think FUSE: Friend, Uncover, Solve, and Execute. Each of the elements will be present in some form and, to some degree, in every successful sales transaction.

Friend

Friending is a digital way of expressing a very old idea. When you "friend" someone, you are getting to know that person, extending a little bit of social trust as you reveal a little bit about yourself. Understand that there are levels of trust and corresponding levels of "friends." As one of our focus group attendees said, "I tell all my real friends, not all the people I know on Facebook. On Facebook, everybody wants to be your friend, but I don't tell everybody everything."

If time is not an issue, the longer you spend in the friending process, the less time you will spend on the remaining three steps. Keep in mind that the Millennials probably will not want to spend too much energy in the friending stage. The Boomers will want more friending, and Gen X will be somewhere in the middle. The trick is knowing when enough is enough.

Here is why the friending step is so important: it makes the next step possible. Unless people feel comfortable with you as an individual, they are not likely to allow you to turn the sales process into the assisting-to-buy exercise we know as invisible selling.

Notice, there is no section or advice on cold calling. Still want that advice? Don't cold call. Fred Vang says, "The closing ratio on cold calling is too low to be valuable. Instead, spend your efforts wowing the customers you already have."

Uncover

In this step, your goal is to find out what the customer wants as well as needs. Every sale has a minimum of one, hopefully two, parties getting their needs met. A customer comes to you for a reason, just as you are in business for a reason. You might think customers would gladly tell you what they want out of the transaction. And you would be wrong!

Because many customers have been the target of high-pressure sales tactics, they may not risk telling their true feelings to a stranger. If you had spent more time friending, maybe it wouldn't be as big an issue. But it is an issue, and all you can do is start over with the friending or gut it out until you have coaxed all the information you can from the customer. If there is one most important tip when it comes to listening to customers, it is this: sweat the small stuff. When a customer notices you noticing the smallest details, she will conclude that you are really listening. Then, and only then, will she risk sharing the details.

The uncover step will not happen without building trust. You are no doubt seeing that in sales, trust is key. One terrific way to build trust is to unsell when appropriate. Unselling is a simple matter of refusing to sell something that is not in the best interest of the customer.

We know it is not right to sell people things they do not need and cannot afford. But it is also not right to sell things that aren't the right solution to the problem customers came to solve. That includes selling too little of what they do want or need, or selling anything they are not going to need or want.

The ultimate reason for the uncover step is to set you up for the third step.

Solve

To be accurate, this step should be labeled "solve *completely*." Here is where you choose between being an order taker and being a sales professional. And here is where you are likely to run into difficulty with the Millennial customer. The Millennials are known to do research before buying, so it is important that your sales staff sells quality solutions that are also complete solutions. This maximizes your sale, and both parties win.

Do not permit a salesperson who sells features rather than benefits to do more than greet a Millennial, or the informed Millennial shopper will begin to have second thoughts. What does it mean to sell features? When you're selling features, you're talking about the product. When you're selling benefits, you're talking about what the product will do for the customer. Feature: "This aircraft has speedbrakes that pop out of the wing." Benefit: "You can slow this plane quickly without shock-cooling the engine." Feature: "The master bath has heated floors." Benefit: "No more need to stand on tiptoe while you are shaving!"

Salespersons have to be able to answer questions and demonstrate knowledge. Once customers question the value of the sales staff, they question the value of the product. Keep in mind that knowledge is often an important part of the solution. That includes on-the-spot training in the form of demonstrating the product. It can also come in the form of FAQ sheets or referrals to websites. Use your imagination!

"Great questions and multiple contacts that focus on solutions dramatically increase the likelihood you will eventually get a sale." —Jack Sims

---

A huge benefit of step three is that there is no reason to close the sale at this point. The customer has described the problem to be solved, and you simply advise him or her what it would take to solve it. The only question left for you to ask is, "Are there any other problems you are working on?"

The ultimate purpose of this step is to roll into position for the final step.

Execute

Execute may be the last step of the FUSE process, or it could be the beginning of the first step again, to continue selling. In this step, we deliver on the promise. Here is your opportunity to justify your price. Now is also the time to educate, expedite, and manage every detail of the experience with the idea of creating compelling, positive word of mouth (whether literal or digital) and setting yourself up for the next sale. All Millennials (really, everybody) love to be entertained, they love a good deal, and this is the step where you can take a little more time to deliver a *wow* that will make your smartphone vibrate the next day with new customers who heard about the great product and service at your place!

In all complete transactions, follow-up should be more about caring than selling. There is a saying that professional platform presenters use: *They don't care how much you know until they know how much you care.* The follow-up also gives you the opportunity to ask customers if they have new concerns that you can help solve.

When it's done right, selling is invisible. Customers are not consciously aware that they are being sold, because they are not. They are being *served* in a transaction where both parties win.

Ignite the Online FUSE

As we know, Millennials spend a lot of time online. You can turn that to your advantage with a skillful, professional sales presentation that takes full advantage of the web's audio and video technology. A web-based sales effort should look more like an in-person presentation than a printed offer. In the best of circumstances, it should simulate a product demo, illustrating complex or possibly hidden benefits, and most importantly featuring high-value testimonials.

Using FUSE as a template, the concepts of personalization and customization fit right in. There is nothing more personal than Friending. The S step (solve the problem completely) is a perfect opportunity to offer a solution that is tailored exactly to the customer and the situation. Above all, use the FUSE acronym as a template, not a boilerplate. Millennials hate canned sales pitches!

Here's how you might use the FUSE process online.

Friend the prospect. Since you are not presenting in person, begin by saying or doing something likely to cause the prospect to like you *personally*: "If you are watching this, chances are that, like me, you enjoy the outdoor lifestyle."

Uncover the problem. Find out what kind of problem the customer is attempting to solve. List a few of the most common problems that customers may identify. Better yet, offer a quiz or a survey, and be sure to involve each customer's results in the solution you recommend: "According to your quiz results, you are concerned about bugs that could infest your pantry and are likely to carry disease. We recommend our Bug-Free Pantry product . . ." or "According to your quiz results, you want your application to be as safe as possible. We recommend our Pantry Perfect bug spray applicator wand."

Solve the problem. Here is where the efficacy of your material will live or die. Tell or show the customer why the problem has not been solved until now: Describe "a revolutionary new compound" or perhaps note that your solution was "discovered by NASA scientists." You get the picture—and that is exactly what your customer should get, visions of the problem successfully solved. Be sure to tackle the objections you might expect if you were selling in person.

"If they hit you with their objections, count yourself lucky. Without objections, there is no sale, because objections define the customer's interest." —Fred Vang

---

Execute. If you did this just right, now is the time to present a complete solution. You are ready to light the fuse by executing, entertaining, educating, and expediting the delivery.

Remember that the web-based pitch should do everything a human in-person sales experience can—or more. A classic example is foodloversfatloss.com, a site so complete that in some respects it's better being there online than in person. The author of the program talks directly to you through the website. You can find testimonials, ideas for getting started . . . the works!

Create a Positive Feeling

Psychologists tell us that all our decisions come down to this: which choice will make me feel good, or at least not make me feel bad? Some believe that we work much harder to avoid pain than to seek pleasure. Smart marketers are constantly asking, where is the pain? Anything you can do or say that makes the customer feel good about saying yes, or avoid feeling bad for saying no, moves you closer to a deal.

If the importance of a chapter was proportionate to the word count, this chapter would be a monster—most of the book. So read this out loud, read it slowly, repeat it time and time again, get a tattoo: *all buying is emotional*. Fred Vang says, "The best way to get a dollar from your customer is to love it out of his pocket."

Getting to Yes

As long as you do it ethically, it is okay to manipulate your customer to a buying decision. Here are nine psychological helpers to get you closer to yes. Fred and I both are fans of Robert Cialdini, author of *Influence, the Psychology of Persuasion*. We have a slightly different take on the items listed below, but Cialdini led the way and we consider him to be the master.

1. Scarcity/exclusivity

2. Contrast

3. Reciprocity

4. Authority/believability

5. Desirability/affinity

6. Comfort or convenience

7. Engagement

8. Consistency

9. Surprise

First is *scarcity/exclusivity*. Smart salespersons know that products in short supply take on greater value in the mind of the customer. If there is not a shortage, it might be a good idea to create one. Exclusivity is a form of scarcity. "Not everyone can be accepted for membership" is received as a challenge to some, and for those who feel that way, price is not going to be an issue. In fact, although we tend to get hung up on customers who want a low price, for a large segment, paying a high price is a badge of honor.

Here are a few scarcity/exclusivity lines you might want to adopt or adapt:

- "You won't see anyone else wearing this dress."
- "This offer expires at noon tomorrow."
- "Tonight I have for dessert . . . "
- "Not everyone can appreciate . . . "

And for Millennials, try, "Your friends are going to want it!"

Second is *contrast*. Value depends on comparison. The law of contrast says that, given the choice between two similar products, customers almost always choose the lower-priced one. When offered the choice between *three* similar products (call it good/better/best), they almost always choose the middle price. If you only have two models, it is good to add a third, higher-priced version in order to make your former higher-priced model now your middle and most-chosen model. Millennials will pay for extra service and enhanced features . . . if you remember to sell the benefits.

Third is *reciprocity*. Reciprocity is the tension we feel when someone does something for us. Even if it is something small, we feel compelled to do something in exchange. Pouring a customer a fresh cup of coffee, offering to give him a lift back to the office, or simply loaning him an umbrella is often all it takes to swing the sales decision in your favor. The theory is simple: a small kindness or concession creates a sense of obligation on the part of the recipient, and often the recipient returns the gesture at a magnitude much greater than the original act. Give a little. Get a lot.

Fred has a favorite story about reciprocity:

> It was hotter than hell the day a friend and I went to a Persian rug dealer. We were pleasantly surprised to be greeted by a beautiful Iranian woman carrying a polished brass tray. On the tray were glasses of iced tea, sweating on the outside, with a small sprig of mint on the lip of each glass. She didn't ask if we wanted tea. She just said, "Enjoy!" as she handed my friend and me each a glass. We knew two things: we weren't likely to leave the store until we had finished our tea, and now we were obligated to at least take time to listen to her presentation.

Fourth is *authority/believability*. "Doctor recommended" and Sally Field saying, "I take Boniva" are examples of authority/believability. David Beckham wearing H&M underwear is the Millennial equivalent to Broadway Joe Namath wearing Hanes pantyhose. Word of mouth shifts into high gear when it comes from someone with authority.

Fifth is *desirability/affinity*. I hope this isn't strictly an American attitude, but sometimes don't you just *want* something? Not something you need. Just something you want. Beyond covering the basics of food and shelter, want often trumps need.

The things we want are often a form of social approval. Humans have a need to be part of something greater than themselves. That's affinity. It drives us to conform and can also drive us to your cash register! A good example is the "Toyota . . . Thinking Green" campaign. The tagline says it all. Because we are thinking green, we are thinking about you. It is a perfectly good way to use affinity to draw customers closer.

Served versus sold? Served wins every time.

Sixth is the promise of *comfort* or *convenience*. It all comes down to this: we just want to feel good. All business is about relieving pain or, to be more positive, providing comfort. Think of a product, any product, and you will see that I am right. Your marketing should always have the promise of comfort or convenience as the leading message.

Convenience is a form of comfort, so you want to include in your message, when possible, the idea that your product or service is easy and convenient to use. You will feel comfortable shopping in our store; you can feel safe using our shopping cart; our multiple locations are convenient to wherever you are.

Seventh is *engagement*. The old-fashioned way to engage customers was primarily a matter of showmanship, giving your product personality, doing anything to attract attention. The Millennial generation hates hokey, hates contrived, and cannot stand the idea of being coerced into performing. You don't have to have a tent and a lion to practice showmanship, nor must you be silly, intrusive, or garish. You only have to get your audience to look your way. Engagement should be a matter of drawing customers in, not dragging them in.

The key to engaging Millennials is making it personal. Millennials don't want a canned speech or a one-size-fits-none sales approach. Let them connect via voice, video, email, text, or smoke signals if you can. Be there when they want to do business, not just when you choose to be available. And when you do sell to Millennials, let them have it their way.

This need for customization and personalization applies doubly when Millennials are put in a sales position. Once, while renting a car, I noticed an enormous badge pinned to the shirt of the rental agent. The badge was the size of a dinner plate and it tugged at her shirt, making the agent look unbalanced. Ever the corporate trainer, I asked, "So what's with the badge?" The young woman slapped her hand to cover the badge, grimaced, and said, "Oh, it's just more hokey crap from corporate!" Don't put your Millennial salespersons in a position where they're embarrassed by you.

Eighth is *consistency*. "You donated $100 last year," the fundraiser reminds you. That is a killer example of consistency at work. People don't want to be wrong, and they certainly don't want to be made uncomfortable by the one who proves them wrong. If I gave $100 last year, surely I have to give at least that same amount this year because if I don't, either I gave too much last year—making me wrong to have donated that amount—or I am not giving enough this year—which also makes me wrong.

Finally, ninth is the possibility of *surprise*. Make me say wow!

It's no secret: I live on Cheez-its. Cheez-its are a complete food. If you are ever going to be stranded on a deserted island, grab the Cheez-its (and an attractive friend!). Once in a while, when I go off to speak, some eagle-eyed client who wants to show me he understands great service leaves a box of Cheez-its in my room. And I always say wow (and work a little harder).

For a few other ideas, check out chapter 7.

When you are in front of the customer, are you selling product, or are you selling yourself? Both, of course. If you do it right, you will earn the customer's trust that day and loyalty for future days. It all comes down to putting the customer ahead of the sale. When you put the customer first, wait for the Karma bus to make the return trip. You won't wait long!

CHAPTER 4

"I'm Not Afraid of Technology"

Millennials live and breathe technology. It's what defines them. In the same way that Boomers tend to view their automobiles as a reflection of their personal power and sex appeal, Millennials view themselves through technology. In focus groups I've led, 25 percent of Millennials say that technology makes them stand out. They say things like this:

- "It's the technology . . . it's second nature to me."

- "My mom has a new iPhone and asks, 'How do you know how to do this?' And I'm thinking, 'How do you *not* know how to do this?' We've grown up with it. I've done computers since I was four!"

- "I just start pushing buttons . . . We can figure things out."

Most Millennials are masters at using technology to keep in touch. This is a key point. In their lifetimes, rapid changes in technology have caused them to master the art of rapid technology adoption. They are fearless when it comes to wringing more utility out of each newly acquired device. While a Millennial is sharing photos wirelessly with a Facebook friend in Ukraine, the Boomer is just discovering, "Hey! This darned thing has a camera, too! Can you believe it?"

I see technology as the great equalizer. For example, the cost of making movies is no longer prohibitive. For under $10,000, sometimes well under, you can be the movie mogul of an independent movie production company—provided you have room in your bedroom to set up your editing computer and store the camera. Even the famous Sundance Film Festival has added a category for no-budget or low-budget films . . . and some are very good!

Don Tapscott, author of *Grown Up Digital*, has given the Millennials a more accurate, although not as interesting, name— the Net Gen—because they conduct their whole lives on the Internet.[8] Tapscott is right on the money. Refer back to the time- line (pages 11–13), and you will begin to see that technology defines this newest generation.

Computer visionary Alan Kay said that technology is "only technology for people who were born before it was invented."[9]

Use Technology to Become Invisible

Your online presence should be centered on being available when and only when the customer wants your attention. The operating phrase is NO HOVERING!

Customers tell us to leave them alone. Don't hover. Be invisible. When I ask a question, give me the right answer quickly, and then go away. Until the Internet came about, this was an impossible situa- tion to win. In a real-world encounter with a cus- tomer, how could we divine if there would be more questions? How could we know when to disappear or reappear? How could we possibly figure that out?

Internet technology to the rescue.

In most retail situations, you can't know exactly when and where you need to be invisible, but selling online is another story. Online, it's possible to become invisible on command. Online, we can appear to answer questions and solve problems, only to vanish into the cloud when we are no longer needed.

Understand and Meet the New Expectations

Technology does more than define the generation; it shapes their expectations.

The customer wants control over whether the decision is part of the experience. And that's not just a Millennial thing. We all want to control our environment; Millennials just want more control.

If you want Millennials to be your customers, ask them to participate. Let them help you shape the offering, and they will become your marketing department! They will be complimented to be asked and grateful for the recognition as a valued, trusted customer.

All of the elements for creating a positive customer experience work equally well in the online environment with one important exception: your customers can hang out with you online. The key words here are *with you*. Use technology, especially social media (next chapter), to monitor your brand (and that of your competitors), and be ready to jump at a moment's notice if you spot a problem.

Nearly everyone in the wired world will recognize the name *Costa Concordia* as the cruise ship that ran aground in the Mediterranean. What the casual observer might not have caught is that the ship was part of Carnival Cruise Corporation. As reported by Glenn Engler in *Advertising Age*, the company's online response or lack thereof was also a disaster.[10] Rather than being transparent and engaging, the company's response was to "take a bit of a break from posting on our social channels." But as Engler points out, "Online never shuts down, and the public traffic only grew more intense and more negative, and Carnival wasn't present to moderate any of it."

Yes, that was an example of how *not* to listen to your customers, but the lessons there for the learning are as clear as the deep blue waters of the Mediterranean Sea.

Do It Right

Online, you can do everything you can do offline, and you can do it faster and usually cheaper. That is the good news . . . and the bad. It is possible to out-shout your detractors when offline. Online, the consumer rules. Communication that used to be one-to-one is now one-to-many. A consumer with a huge database of friends or followers can be your best friend or your worst nightmare, which is all the more reason you need to cultivate a responsive online presence.

Millennials will tell you the following:

- "Don't speak to me in canned messages. If you want me to listen, speak directly to me, and at least make the pretense that your marketing will be noninvasive. Off-the-shelf marketing is an invasion of my personal space. I don't want to be on your broadcast mailing list. I don't mind that you sent something to your entire database, which included me, but if I feel that you are not address-ing my personal needs, you will not hear from me again!"

- "Treat me as an individual, and give me a sign that you know whom you are talking to. Use my name to show that I was meant to be the recipient."

- "Above all, don't lurk in the shadows. If you are present, don't hide. Make your presence known, and stay out of the conversation unless or until you are invited in. Then do your thing and step back out. Be more or less trans-parent, but don't be creepy!"

Technorati and Google will provide you with targeted, impor-tant information that's customized to you. Amazon recommends books based on what you have ordered in the past and what read-ers "like you" are purchasing. Dodge.com lets you build *your* car online, Domino's will deliver your pizza just the way you like it, and Nimble will monitor the web and jump in if they see you strug-gling with a problem.

The key is to personalize and customize your product for your customers without making your customers feel like you were "just filling in the blanks."

Use Networks

Have you ever heard of the Teltschik family? My guess is you have not, but with a little help from Facebook, you could probably find a Teltschik in short order. Not long ago, more than three hundred

Teltschiks from around the country and across the globe visited our small town for a family reunion. The mayor asked if I could cover for him, so one day I found myself greeting all three hundred Teltschiks in several languages and making an official proclamation that June 18 was "Teltschik Familientag" in Kerrville, Texas.

One necessary task of the Familientag was to prepare for the next. Acutely aware of changing generations, the older members of the group took great pains to invite the Millennials and Gen X to take over the planning of future reunions, which are held every five years, alternating between the US and Germany. The woman who followed me on the program mentioned the countless letters and phone calls required to coordinate such an affair and urged the upcoming leadership to persevere in spite of the effort required.

At lunch after the event, several Boomers from the audience remarked how difficult it might prove to plan an intercontinental trip in a time-pressed world. But the Millennials were not thinking that at all. They were thinking, "Haven't you heard about Skype? Don't you know about translate.com? Have you forgotten about Travelocity?"

The Millennials in attendance had already formed a community long before anyone even thought about travel arrangements. Rather than feeling overly challenged, they were thinking, "Dude! This is going to be awesome!"

The message is clear: networks are everywhere. They form (and dissolve) of their own volition. Watch for them. Be prepared to take advantage of them. No matter what your generation, be open to learning from someone younger.

Don't Forget about Traditional Marketing

It is easy to get caught up in the excitement of something new and worthy of exploration such as social marketing. But social marketing has not yet made traditional marketing obsolete. There remain very good reasons and venues for traditional advertising and marketing, as you will see in figure 6. For example, look at the electronics category. Social media has a much greater influence on Millennials than Boomers (28.7 vs. 8.0). If you looked only at those numbers, you might conclude that social media is the key to the Millennial heart—and you would be wrong. Look to the top of the chart; the greatest influence is in-store promotion for all generations.

For clothing purchases, in-store promotion slightly leads the longtime favorite, word of mouth. Traditional media is getting harder to find as broadcasters and print outlets are becoming ever more adept at integrating social media into traditional marketing campaigns.

Which media influence your purchase decision when buying . . .	Millennials	Gen X	Boomers
Electronics			
In-store promotion	46.9%	39.3%	32.6%
Internet advertising	39.8%	27.6%	22.6%
Social media	28.7%	14.3%	8.0%
Apparel/clothing			
Word of mouth	36.4%	37.5%	32.3%
In-store promotion	39.5%	43.0%	39.6%
Social media	20.0%	12.0%	5.3%
Grocery			
Word of mouth	34.8%	39.7%	38.0%
In-store promotion	36.8%	51.2%	58.3%
Internet advertising	17.3%	15.4%	12.6%
Social media	14.8%	10.8%	5.5%

Source: BIGinsight™, Media Behaviors & Influence Study *(Worthington, OH: Prosper Business Development, 2011).*

Figure 6: Influence of various media.

What do you think? Is traditional media dead? Dying? In transition? I think traditional media still has a big role to play, at least for now. While you are diving into social media, don't forget there is still plenty of play in traditional media. The smart players will use them both, working together.

I can't wait until this concept grows really big. Imagine: I'm in Tuscaloosa, speaking at a conference, when I am notified that fellow speaker Tim Durkin is at Dreamland eating their world famous barbeque. I rush to Dreamland, answer the magic question, "Six or twelve ribs?" and even though I arrive too late for Tim to pay, I don't mind because Amex gives me an award credit for trying. Is this a great country or what?!

Technology begat social media. Social media happened because the technology was there and someone said, why not? In a blink of an eye, web-based technologies turned individuals from narrowcasters to broadcasters with untold leverage. It's a watershed change for communicating, and therefore for reaching potential customers. It's such a big change, in fact, that we need a whole chapter to do it justice. Keep reading.

CHAPTER 5

"I Live through Social Media"

The big social media players, such as Twitter and Facebook, were created to encourage personal relationships—what used to be called networking (or, to some people, golf). To be candid, networking has not always been seen as a desirable talent. The saying "It isn't what you know, it's who you know" suggests, for example, that you can substitute glad-handing for competence.

And then a shift occurred. Suddenly, we were all on Facebook, friending people we otherwise wouldn't let in our house. Malcolm Gladwell wrote *The Tipping Point* and showed how we are all connected, closer than we imagined, LinkedIn and thoroughly friended.

How did this happen? Did humans have difficulty communicating in 1950, 1970, 1980, or 1990? Do we really need constant status updates? Enter social media, with web-based technologies intended to turn one-to-many communication into one-to-one dialogue. In other words, we went from being individual gossipers to spokespersons, even if you were the only member of your group. Social media gives power to the solo voice and replaces speculation with communication. It's the only context in which the idea of a group of one doesn't seem silly.

Increasingly, businesses have recognized social media as an opportunity to build relationships with customers and potential customers. While social media does not solve a specific problem, it does present new opportunities. It is a powerful marketing tool with both good and dangerous characteristics. For the first time, the dialogue of business has changed from company-to-customer to customer-to-customer (see fig. 7, page 60).

2010 Online Communities/Social Media (Facebook, Twitter, and so on)

Millennials	Gen X	Boomer	All Adults
38.1%	24.7%	11.2%	19.6%

Source: *BIGinsight™*, Media Behaviors & Influence Study *(Worthington, OH: Prosper Business Development, 2011).*

Figure 7: Social media users.

Here are more reasons why social media is no longer an opt-out choice. The new generation expects it. Millennials place a high value on having and using the latest technology. Just as carpenters like to have good tools, Millennials treat their corporate technology as a badge of honor. (In fact, we *all* like to be seen as cool people doing cool things.) And Millennials pride themselves in knowing how to use the current tools.

Wouldn't it be great if the folks in the C-suites had a way to keep their fingers on the pulse of the company without feeling as though they are stifling your creativity by their presence? Well, you can do that with social media. And while the folks in the C-suites are listening to get a feel for how things are throughout the company, they are gathering the information needed to transmit the communication necessary to build and maintain a strong corporate culture.

Jon Ferrara is a genius.

He's also an aggressive salesman reminiscent of the Fuller Brush sales reps who would knock on our doors back in the 1950s. Whoever heard of a salesperson knocking on your door?! Well, youngster, there was a time when salesmen did knock, bringing their goods to stay-at-home moms, making the sale from the privacy of their front porches: milk and other dairy products, baked goods, fruit and vegetables, vacuum cleaners, awnings, carpet, aluminum siding, even life insurance. Sales were made on the basis of the seller's ability to establish a relationship with the customer.

In that respect, not much has changed. Sales are *still* made based on your ability to establish and cultivate a relationship with your customer.

Meet Jon Ferrara, founder of Nimble. Jon Ferrara is a genius—and a noticer. The founder of GoldMine, the customer relationship management (CRM) system that was the hit of the 1990s, Ferrara noticed that CRM systems, his included, turned salespersons into data-entry clerks. He also noticed that CRM systems seemed to focus more on generating reports of communications with customers than on developing relationships through actual communications. So Ferrara created Nimble with the express purpose of managing relationships rather than data.

In a telephone interview that left me struggling to keep up, speaking with the passion of an evangelist at a tent revival, Ferrara told me, "Business is social. People buy from people they like, and they like people who know them. And everybody likes to talk about themselves."

What Ferrera noticed that was so important was that most salespeople have to go to Twitter, Facebook, LinkedIn, and other social media sites if they truly want to communicate with their customers. So why not channel those data streams into a single source of valuable customer data?

In Nimble, he said, "We bring it all together and create a single record that you can operate from. I can see [customers'] history. I know if they are following me and who they are following. I can send a message on the channel that the customer can hear me on. I can see who is talking about my product or services. I can see who is saying what on our Facebook page."

Using Nimble, Jon Ferrara can see a lot of things. But I believe what he mostly sees is the future.

Understand the Power of Social Media

Call them facts or factoids, here's proof that social media is key to any marketing campaign:

- Brad Keselowski, a NASCAR driver at the red flag–delayed 2012 Daytona 500 reported via live Tweet from inside his custom Dodge Charger.[11]

- Blendtec quintupled sales after a YouTube campaign.[12]

- 47 percent of small businesses use no social media.[13]
- 60 percent of social networkers are writing reviews and sharing them with friends.[14]

If these stats are enough to get you interested, consider these ways you can use social media to your advantage:

- **Educate the marketplace about new products—** Sometimes all you have to do is post and let the market come to you. Ford's pre-release social media campaign for the Fiesta netted six and a half million YouTube views and 50,000 requests for information. Brand awareness was so high, the company sold 10,000 Fiestas in the first six days.[15]

  In our office, Buns's favorite forum is Live Community. Open the software Quickbooks, and you'll see a link to it on the right of your screen for quick access to solutions for any problem already experienced by other users. One of the coolest (and most reassuring) features is the Leaderboard, where those who take the time to help others earn points and a status on the Top Ten Contributors List. That's recognition for being a Quickbooks user, and it lightens the load of the help desk folks at Intuit. You can have a learning experience often without having to experience the problem!

- **Provide support to multiple customers simultaneously—**View the Internet as a stage where the audience potential is unlimited. Because of its public nature, any action you take to help one customer has a huge potential to spill over to others with no additional investment of time required.

- **Intercept customer complaints—**If you can gracefully intercept a complaint, you are on the way to saving a call center transaction and saving a customer in the process. Intercepted complaints are golden opportunities to wow the customer with a little Positively Outrageous Service. If your intercept allows you to give preemptive support by solving problems before they escalate, all the better.

Long before you interrupt a conversation to offer assistance or intercept your first complaint, it is critical that you develop and enforce a set of hard-and-fast rules for your team. You need to make sure that you avoid the creepiness factor, so your company won't be branded a social media vulture. If you are monitoring a conversation, reveal both your presence and your full identity. If you are a serious online business, you will want to adopt standards for handling self-help abandons, shopping cart abandons, and customers who might benefit from a chat to guide them to a solution. Adopt the standards, and stick to them.

I take my lead from my friends at Sitel, the experts in call center management. Sitel says the goal is to "capture the customer's interest and engage the customer at the most appropriate time." Their intention is to "handpick the best customer moments." The idea is not to intercept every call but rather to *select* the calls that are most leverageable in terms of influencing the customer base as a whole.

As for web-monitoring rules of your own, these tips will start you thinking:

- Staff the effort with knowledgeable product advocates (people who *love* the product).

- Define the objective for each category of intercept in measureable terms.

- Avoid engaging customers who are likely to use self-service or unlikely to buy.

- Base your strategies on how your customers use the web and social media.

The key to having an online presence is quick if not immediate response. How a complaint is handled is usually more important than the incident that triggered the complaint. It is important to move fast and move fairly. If the complainer is clearly a now-satisfied customer, do not miss the opportunity to subtly ask that person to add his or her story to your testimonials.

- **Sell . . . but only if it can be done in the natural course of the conversation**—Remember, you are on social media, not QVC. Keep the FUSE process in mind (chapter 3, page 42), and solve the problem completely while keeping the social media social.

- **Gather marketing intelligence**—Surveys are made to order for social media, as long as you offer something of value in return, often nothing more than to share the results. One avenue of research for this book was a simple survey associated with my blog on Forbes. com. The survey was short and cost next to nothing, but pointed me in the right direction when I planned focus groups.

- **Recruit vendors**—Watch for B2B partnerships that might work for you, and ask to be included in the club.

- **Attract new customers as well as new employees**—Keep in mind that you are using *social* media, which was created originally for building relationships, not for marketing. Respect that boundary, and think "invisible" while you let your target audience come to you.

- **Listen to your fans**—Celebrate them. Let them tell their stories. Make them feel like family, and you will build loyalty and positive word of mouth. Establish a listening base where you can gather fan input and transfer ownership of the brand to your fans.

"Once a relationship is established, no one wants to disappoint!"
—Fred Vang

Market with Social Media

If you are a small business owner and are ready to begin using social media in your business, do this:

- **Target your audience**—Your marketing will be more effective if first you define the individual you want most to reach; it could be your current best customers or prospects you would most like to reach. Give your target a name. Give her a personality, give her a little history, and think of her as if she is a living, breathing representation of the people you want to attract.

  For example, your ideal customer might be Amanda Smith, age thirty-four, with two children and a household income of $80,000. She likes to read, speaks some French, and exercises regularly.

- **Be 100 percent open**—If you are a business, then make it clear. The Internet is a dangerous place to make false claims.

- **Begin with specific results in mind**—Decide up front what your goals are. Do you want to build awareness, increase trial, boost short-term sales, or recruit new employees? I believe Stephen Covey says to begin with the end in sight. It is much easier to hit a goal when you know what it is!

- **Ask your customers to help**—Find out what other sites your customers visit, and develop a strategy for luring them to your site—or join them where they already are going.

- **Get started**—Facebook and Twitter should be early targets. They are by far the most popular, plus they are easy to use. Let the 140-character limit of Twitter work in your favor: it's easier and less time-consuming than writing lengthy copy.

- **Learn the differences**—Facebook users are all ages; LinkedIn users tend to be older and more professional. While Facebook conversations are what you might hear at a family barbeque, LinkedIn communications are what you might hear at a business convention.

Let's look at two companies that use social media to market to the new customers, the Millennials.

Sony

While watching the X Games playing on the widescreen TV at Mimi's Restaurant, we couldn't help but notice the low-key Sony commercials that invited us to come a little closer to the brand. As a sponsor using traditional marketing, we were led to the Sony site on Facebook, Sony on YouTube, and Sony on Flickr. Along the way, we discovered opportunities for Sony-loving photographers to show off their talents, as well as their Sony equipment. (I have the NEX-VG10 ... killer!) All were nonintrusive, the no-pitch pitch! Sony is known for being a company of vision, but how has it been able to magnify that vision to continue to compete globally? Here's the inside scoop.

Sony got a surprisingly late start on social media, led by a small group of Sony employees who decided in 2007 that it was time for Sony to join the move to social media. After dutifully going through the channels, these employees were told that the time was not right for investing resources in something so few inside Sony knew any-thing about. Fortunately for Sony, these rebels realized the com-pany couldn't wait for approvals and forged ahead. They recognized the need for the URLs and the accounts, and put their stake in the ground—which turned out to be a good thing because it led to recruiting Sukhjit Ghag.

Sukhjit helped me with her name, pronounced sook-jeet. It means "happiness" in Punjabi (a dialect of India and Pakistan). The name suits her!

"I was a blogger," she said. "I came from traditional broadcast and . . . have always loved technology . . . the gadgets and innovations. I created my own presence online, and when Sony put the word out for a social media evangelist, they found me. That title came with the job. Fifty percent is evangelizing to the fans and the other fifty percent of the time I visit and listen to the company, showing them how important social media is to them."

While at Sony, her title was social media evangelist, which fits as perfectly as her name. Both communicate promises of enthusiasm, and Sukhjit does not disappoint.

"I know it sounds silly," she says, "but I get excited when people get excited . . . that moment when you meet a fan. I am still surprised at how many people want to meet us around the country. They are so excited, so sweet and amazed that they would have an opportunity to talk with a big company. They are surprised to be touched by a brand and the real people that work there."

According to Sukhjit, the next big thing at Sony will be when social media will no longer be considered something out of the ordinary, but will become second nature in all of the departments. She's looking forward to a time when "everyone in the company knows that this way of reaching out is not fringe or being an early adopter . . . when social media is not a category . . . when even hiring practices will be adopted that will help you go about finding people who are passionate about our brand."

In her mind, that would be Sukhjit! (You can follow Sukhjit at blog .sony.com/author/Sukhjit.)

Southwest Airlines

It wasn't until I had ended my call with Christy McNeill that it occurred to me that companies belong to generational cohorts, too. Southwest Airlines (SWA) is definitely Millennial. I should have realized that right away. I'm a Boomer. I flew SWA when the flight attendants were stewardesses in hot pants. I have SWA drink coupons that are older than my grandkids! But just because SWA has been around a while doesn't mean the company is a Boomer like me. I really should have known a Millennial company when I saw one.

Christy is an emerging media specialist, part of the SWA social media team. What started as a corporate blog has grown into a full-fledged department. Somebody in the SWA IT department is a genius. SWA, if you remember, led the industry in ticketless travel. When other airlines were still issuing printed tickets at the counter, SWA customers were checking in online. So it is no surprise that SWA would grab the lead in social media in the airline industry.

- Seven out of ten Facebook users are outside the United States.
- Three out of four Millennials have a profile on social media and one in five has posted a video.

Sources: Burbary 2011; Pew Research Center 2010.

Adept at creating fun and interesting campaigns, they even use Twitter and Facebook for crisis communications. Their next big idea is to use social media as a tool to communicate with their workforce.

"Do people really want a relationship with an airline?" I asked Christy.

"It depends on the airline!" she replied. "The big surprise was that our customers really do want a relationship with an airline . . . if it is Southwest! They like our fun and quirky attitude, and when we don't reflect that in our social media, they are quick to remind us. . . . We have our own personality, and customers enjoy connecting with us on a personal level. Any one of our employees who writes a blog has their own photo and bio. I think our customers enjoy hearing Southwest stories from Southwest employees. That even applies to the commercials you see on TV . . . we use real Southwest employees. It's a personal touch that you don't find with other brands.

"We receive way more compliments and general kudos than we do complaints. The challenge is being able to thank all the customers who tweet us or email us to share their great customer service experience, or to show us a picture of their flight."

That's a great problem to have!

"There is a generation of people coming out of college this year who are not aware of life before Facebook," she explained. "If they have a great experience on Southwest and want to share, they turn to Facebook. Other generations are more comfortable writing a letter to our CEO."

"Is it expensive?" I wondered.

"Even though we have devoted headcount and resources to the media, you can still do a lot with a little."

SWA has a history of giving freedom and latitude to employees, and I wanted to explore that subject without using the word *control*. I asked Christy whether they had run into problems of inappropriate postings.

"Our brand and the way we do things aren't for everyone," she acknowledged. "We have been working on creating policies for our employees about how they can use social media. As a company, we see our employees as a great resource who like to share their SWA experience online. A lot of it is just common sense."

It's sort of Mom's Rules for Running an Airline. Why am I not surprised?

Grow the Program

Here are a few tips to consider before you begin your social media program:

- Social media is small talk on a very public platform, so mind your manners.

- Deliver content, not sales pitches.

- Provide content in a variety of modes that your customers will appreciate (audio, video, text, surveys, games, and so on).

- If you can't field a team of tech-savvy employees, stay out of the game, or get yourself to classes. Better yet, hire a student.

When you are comfortably proficient (you'll know when that is), consider expanding by doing the following:

- **Monitor social media forums**—The benefits outlined previously will automatically manifest themselves.

- **Build online communities and forums as part of your website**—Don't hesitate to get outside professional help, and don't even think about launching unless you or a staff member can reliably dedicate the time needed to respond consistently.

Don't forget to mind your own business. Your website is a virtual store, and just like with a brick-and-mortar store, you have to have sufficient, well-trained, carefully selected staff to monitor the communication.

Spread the Word

Remember, we need to give our customers something positive to talk about. If you want to generate positive, compelling word of mouth, you must earn it.

In marketing, there's nothing more powerful than one customer recommending you to another customer.

This is where social media exerts incredible pressure. There is no more powerful testimonial than one delivered by a trusted friend or, at the very least, someone related to someone you know.

With social media, we can influence what our new customers (Millennials) are going to say to other potential customers. Millennials "report" to their friends and family how good or bad their customer service experience was, the minute it happens, on Facebook and Twitter. They do not see themselves as complaining online; they are just "warning friends."

In the August 2011 issue of *Fast Company*, Lady Gaga expressed her devotion to her fans—thirty-five million Facebook friends and ten million Twitter followers. When she released her new album this year, so many responded that Amazon's servers crashed.

Here are five tips for marketing with social media, straight from the latest master representing Millennials everywhere:

1. Target like-minded individuals. Do not target the demographic. Start with a common interest, like music was for Lady Gaga and her fans.

2. Be vulnerable.

3. Treat the consumer like your boss. This helps you understand them and therefore evolve along with them.

4. Create a collective experience (which she does with social media).

5. Become a better company through community.

Have a Conversation

Social media could be described as a virtual meeting space where you can hang out with your customers. Your virtual address should be a place where customers can come to play, learn, and share . . . when they want to.

Social media is a gift to capitalists because, when used properly, it helps lower the cost of customer service, making you more efficient, more profitable, and therefore more competitive. (And that's important when dealing with the bargain-hunting Millennials.)

For instance, an effective social media effort can lower costs by reducing expensive call center staffing and equipment. By monitoring online conversations, call center web-watchers can join an online conversation that is not going well and quite literally save the day—and the customer! Online interceptions, handled properly, are a great marketing opportunity with vast potential for improving the efficiency of delivering great customer service. For social media to work in your favor, you have to be committed; otherwise it can bite you.

For example, one in eight banking customers report attempting to use social media to contact their bank.[16] Of that group, only 20 percent reported getting an answer! And 47 percent of those who use social media to contact their bank expect to continue to use the bank. Of customers who attempt contact and get no reply, however, only 27 percent indicate they will remain with the bank.

Commit! Get all the way in or all the way out.

What you just read is a primer on why to use social media. Now how about we head to the good stuff and see what happens when a Millennial gets a dose of his own media!

CHAPTER 6

"I Want It My Way"

Remember the Millennial mantra from earlier in the book? "My way, right away, why pay?"

You're dealing with the smartest, most well-informed customers you've ever known. Millennials do their homework before deciding on a purchase, they know exactly what they want and what it should cost, and they are not afraid to negotiate. And they don't want to wait.

Expect Prepurchase Research

When a Millennial walks into your store or visits your website, he or she comes armed with lots of information. Before you even see them, Millennials have done deep research (see fig. 8). They know all there is to know about your products and, to a large extent, even your costs. You can't fool them with fancy footwork, and if they sense that the sales staff doesn't know the product as well as they do, they're out the door.

Research Online: Over the last ninety days, which types of products did you research online before buying them in person?	Millennials	All
Apparel	22.9%	21.3%
Appliances	24.1%	19.1%
Beauty Care/Cosmetics	14.7%	13.9%
Car/Truck	13.1%	11.0%
Electronics	44.9%	40.6%
Food/Groceries	13.9%	13.6%
Furniture	13.0%	11.1%

continued →

Research Online: Over the last ninety days, which types of products did you research online before buying them in person?	Millennials	All
Home Decor	15.0%	12.1%
Home Improvement Items	19.4%	14.8%
House/Land	3.8%	3.1%
Jewelry/Watches	10.0%	8.9%
Medicines/Vitamins/Supplements	16.1%	14.2%
Shoes	19.5%	17.9%
Tires/Batteries/Auto Parts	12.3%	10.3%
Other	8.4%	9.1%

Source: BIGinsight™, Media Behaviors & Influence Study *(Worthington, OH: Prosper Business Development, 2011).*

Figure 8: Online products research.

If you ask Millennials which media has influence over their purchase decisions, in almost every category—from radio to TV, blogs to billboards—they claim they are *more* influenced than Gen X or Boomers (see fig. 9, page 73). However, when everything ranks high as an influence, then maybe nothing is a true influence. The numbers lead us to a few standouts:

- Overall, social media doesn't seem to have a great impact on purchase decisions, but when it has an impact, that impact seems greatest with Millennials.

- Newspaper has more impact than social media for commodity purchases such as groceries.

- It's evident that while social media is the current hot button, even Millennials don't rank it at the top for influencing their purchase decisions. Now wait a minute, you might be thinking, didn't we just spend a chapter talking about how social media matters? I've managed to aggravate a few clients and at least one editor with the seeming contradiction between this chapter and the last. I admit it has bothered me as well. The fact is, I'm writing this book today, not tomorrow. And today, social media has yet to become the final media answer. In some instances, traditional media trumps social media—today. I can only guess about tomorrow, but my best guess is that the only change you will see in this argument is the relative numbers.

Which media influence your purchase decision when buying ...	Millennials	Gen X	Boomers
Electronics			
Word of mouth	44.3%	45.1%	41.9%
In-store promotion	46.9%	39.3%	32.6%
Internet advertising	39.8%	27.6%	22.6%
Social media	28.7%	14.3%	8.0%
Apparel/clothing			
Word of mouth	36.4%	37.5%	32.3%
In-store promotion	39.5%	43.0%	39.6%
Internet advertising	27.9%	22.6%	16.9%
Social media	20.0%	12.0%	5.3%
Grocery			
Coupons	53.7%	67.3%	73.4%
Word of mouth	34.8%	39.7%	38.0%
In-store promotion	36.8%	51.2%	58.3%
Internet advertising	17.3%	15.4%	12.6%
Social media	14.8%	10.8%	5.5%

Source: BIGinsight™, Media Behaviors & Influence Study *(Worthington, OH: Prosper Business Development, 2011).*

Figure 9: Media influences for electronics, apparel, and grocery.

From figure 9, we can see that:

- Millennials are more likely to respond to Internet ads, social media, and in-store promotions.

- For clothing purchases, the heavy lifting for all groups remains word of mouth and in-store promotions. Think of social media as high-tech word of mouth.

- Millennials aren't nearly as likely as Boomers to use coupons for grocery purchases. Why? Because grocery coupons are most often found in the newspaper.

Deliver Options

Millennials are kings of customization. They truly want, and expect, to have it their way. With Millennials, you can expect flexible delivery of service and product to be the rule rather than the exception. Successful companies will look for every opportunity to custom-tailor the service as well as the product. In my own business, speaking (a lot) and consulting (some—it's not as fun as speaking), notice that I have even taken my own advice! Here's an excerpt from my website showing my "flexible delivery options."

Traditional keynote

- Short, entertaining, no PowerPointless
- Requires full stage wash, wireless lavalier microphone

Conversational keynote

- Slightly longer, nonscripted, audience directs content
- You choose the topic . . . let your audience choose the content!
- Lots of light, wireless lavalier microphone, stool

Break-out session

- Hands on, Scott gives in and resorts to limited PowerPoint.
- Must be properly lighted for PPT . . . no dungeon rooms!

Scott a la Carte!

Feel free to mix topics. Half-day bookings are ideal for a keynote followed by an application session, but you are welcome to order two back-to-back general session presentations (same or different topic).

Have it your way!

Online retailers! Yes, I am talking to you. You have plenty of product information, so why not make it useful and available to the customer? How about providing the ability to screen share when shopping online? This feature can allow shoppers to assemble their research in a format most useful to them, and that is right up the Millennial alley.

Prepare to Negotiate

Millennials negotiate everything. And they know how to pull a deal apart. They will calmly ask for consideration on such "extras" as free delivery, service contracts, extended warranties, extra training time, extended technical support, and anything else they can think of.

Remember that kid in chapter 2 who said, "I bargain everywhere. I go to customer service and ask for at least 10 percent off"? He's certainly not alone, and so you had best be ready. When you're on the other end of that kind of negotiation, here are a few tips to make negotiating a bit more civilized:

- Avoid presenting to a group of customers, as individuals will look to others for cues and possibly end up doing nothing. In-person presenting to a group is difficult. Online, it is deadly. This is mainly due to the anonymity that comes from hiding behind a keyboard.

- Find out what the other side values early in the process, if not before.

- Establish your expertise.

- Start with small commitments and build. The idea is to establish the feeling of "we have worked too hard to back away now."

- It is better to bargain hard from the beginning. If you hold back a few concessions for the other party to win, they will feel like they were part of the negotiation and will be more committed to the deal. Leading with your best offer sets an artificially low starting point. Recognize that some people feel psychologically compelled to negotiate, so leave them some room. Millennials are culturally predisposed to haggling. Let them haggle, but start high enough that you'll be satisfied with the outcome.

- Use product as a bargaining tool as it adds full-price value while you only pay the wholesale price. If you really need to bargain, bargain equal value for value, not equal dollars for value. In a web-based business or stick-built retail outlet, you have delivery, training and support, future discounts, and accessories to use as value-enhancing offers. The key is to remember when you trade value for value, you are giving at wholesale and getting at retail.

On the other hand, we also know that given sufficient motivation, Millennials will pay extra for great customer service. In fact, they will pay a premium for service that is worthy of a premium charge. (If you're not sure whether your service is up to that level, it probably isn't. You'll find some good ideas in chapter 7.)

Those two elements—customization and paying for extra value—go into smart negotiations. For instance:

- Do you offer delivery?
- Is delivery free?
- Can I pay extra for expedited delivery?
- Does the price include setup?
- And if I don't require that service, do I get a discount?
- If you are making a call to my home and office, can I pay extra for you to guarantee your arrival time?
- If I bring my kitchen appliance, my cat, or my sore throat to you, do I get a discount since you no longer have travel time as an expense?

Unbundle Your Service

More and more retailers are answering the My Way mantra by unbundling service from the mix. (Stores like Sam's Club and Costco are not as affected by this trend, as they never really had service factored into their costs in the first place. They have taught customers that there are many products for which there is no useful service component. Just stack 'em deep and sell 'em cheap. You

don't need service with dish soap in gallon jugs or cotton bale–
sized packages of toilet paper.)

If you are going to unbundle product from your customer service, you had better get good at tangibilizing. (If *tangibilizing* is not
a word, it should be.) Here is the meaning: if you do something
for a customer and the customer does not know you did it, did you
do it? NO! You added to the cost but failed to add to the value. So
start tangibilizing!

While I have you talking to yourself, you might want to ask,
"Am I adding value that my customers will pay for?" Pay attention
here. Unbundling only works if (1) your service is worth the premium and (2) the customer is fully aware of the process and the
reasoning behind it.

You could take the old-fashioned, all-or-nothing approach, or
you could get with the program and sell your customer service
options and customization as accessories. For example, a dentist
could unbundle standard service by offering run-of-schedule teeth
cleaning. Sign up to be a run-of-schedule patient, and if someone
cancels their appointment, you get a discount for filling in. (Get
it?) The dentist avoids an empty, non-revenue-producing chair, and
you get rewarded for being flexible.

Watch for your cell service to become unbundled. In the
United States, mobile phone penetration is more
than 90 percent, which leaves stealing market share
the only way to achieve meaningful growth. So
what is likely to happen? Not only will you be able
to save by buying only the services you want, but
carriers will be able to pitch the pieces you want at
greatly discounted prices through limited-term offers.

If you have the best product, but the customer doesn't know it, you have no advantage.

Do customers understand unbundling? According to J.D.
Power and Associates, they do. They note that as dissatisfaction
with banking fees is decreasing, overall satisfaction is finally mov-
ing in the right direction: "Customers who completely understand
their bank's fee structure and value the products and services they

receive tend to have higher overall satisfaction, despite paying fees," says Michael Beird.[17]

Don't Make Them Wait

Just as they expect that all things are possible, Millennials expect everything to be fast. (Believe it or not, there are home furnishing stores named Get It Now.) The concept of waiting for anything is totally foreign and unnecessary to them. Who wants to wait? Who needs to wait when there is fast food and texting, and haven't you heard of FedEx?

Remember the Critical Service Points

Here, listed in David Letterman order, are the five points consumers told us were most critical to them. You might think of it as a kind of summary of everything we've learned so far about these "My Way" Millennials.

5. A Fast Finish

Customers have two common moods when on a shopping expedition: the buying mood and the leaving mood. Once customers are no longer in the buying mood, they quickly shift to the leaving mood. You can make them an offer at the checkout or even tempt them with impulse items, but you do so at your own peril. As the folks at Chili's might say, "Get in. Get out. Get on with your life!"

If you want to irritate a customer *intentionally*, the best way would be to have too few checkout lines staffed with cashiers who are on their cell phones with a friend.

Here is the deal. Americans are among the hardest-working people in the world. We work on average 1,979 hours per year, which is up thirty-six hours since 1990. Why is this statistic important?

In an online environment, this applies to pop-ups that appear when an order is abandoned. "Are you sure you want to leave this page?" Yes, I'm sure!

"But I recover such a high percentage of those I intercept!" say the online companies. I say to them, have you figured out how many customers get turned off and never return?

4. Ease and Convenience

Customers want you to be convenient and easy to do business with. They want you to be open when they want to shop. They want you to accept their methods of payment, offer delivery and other ancillary services, and above all be visually customer friendly on things such as signage, adjacencies, and parking.

Oddly enough, there's a list of online equivalents. Good signage translates to an efficient search capability, for example. The online match to convenient parking is a site design that gets you to the department you want without delay.

Demonstrate that your customers are important by respecting their time.

3. Price That Represents a Value

Notice that our survey participants did not ask for a low price. They asked for a price that represents a value.

If price is an issue with your customers, you may be attempting a customer-product offer that is not going to work. Before you throw in the towel, ask yourself, "Have I been talking features, or have I been demonstrating benefits?" A good demonstration of the benefits lets the product do most of the selling. If you aren't offering taste tests or free trials, you may be limiting the success of a good offer.

Here is a question for you. What do you already do for your customers that would add value if they knew you were doing it? Use the opportunity to tangibilize! Tell them if the chicken is free-range. Tell them if your technicians are certified. Let them know if that toilet seat is sanitized for their protection. Because if you don't tell them what you are doing on their behalf, you are adding to the cost without adding to the value.

2. Friendly, Likable Staff

People like to do business with people they like. Duh! In the best of all circumstances, your customers prefer to do business with people who share their core values. Think about that when you hire and train your staff. (More about this in chapter 8.)

1. Knowledgeable, Available Staff

The number-one element of a successful transaction is staff who are knowledgeable and available when the customer wants them. Our respondents told us they want help on their terms, and that includes *not* having staff "hovering when you don't need them." Customers also told us flat out that a salesperson who cannot answer their questions is Worthless with a capital W. The reason customers negotiate is that they don't understand what they are getting for their money.

You may have also noticed that your salespersons must be well versed in the culture of your company and able to sell to people of different generations.

What do they want?

- Traditionals will be concerned about price and quality.

- Boomers will want to talk about quality and service.

- Gen X will talk quality and will want to negotiate the price.

- Millennials want quality, price, *and* service. They won't take no for an answer, and they will shop until they find the deal that wins on all three.

In this chapter, we learned five things a customer wants from a service transaction. On the surface, these seem like easy things to deliver, and you know what? They are. In our next chapter, you will get a close-up look at what we call Positively Outrageous Service. POS requires a little imagination, but it can make the difference in brick-and-mortar stores as well as online. Why? Because everyone loves a surprise!

CHAPTER 7

"Surprise Me"

You might think that *nothing* surprises these quick-thinking, quick-talking, ultra-hip Millennials. And probably very little does. That's why when you *do* manage to surprise them, the impact is huge. And unforgettable. So, do I really need to tell you to make sure the surprise is a positive one?

Deliver Positively Outrageous Service

How would you define customer service? I say customer service is a product manufactured one customer at a time in the presence of the buyer.

This is why it is so important to deliver good, if not great, customer service. If you fail to deliver, it can cause many undesired negative results: loss of customers, loss of sales, loss of your good employees (who do not want to play on a losing team), and worst of all, the loss of being a respected brand leader.

Because it is a one-of-a-kind product, you cannot deliver great customer service from a script. Millennials do not like being treated like a number. Who does?

Some of you might know me as the author of *Positively Outrageous Service*. Those who practice Positively Outrageous Service usually refer to the concept as POS. And we are thankful that many refer to the book as a "management classic." POS was one of those bass-ackward discoveries where the instruction manual was written around the practices in the field. It is a long story that essentially describes how we turned a losing restaurant business into a winner and looked back to find out how we did it so we could write the manual for doing it again.

Audiences and readers around the world said, "Wow, what a concept!" That thought was quickly replaced by, "Hey! That is what I am already doing when things are going right. POS isn't a new idea at all!"

I already knew that. (One of the learned skills from my corporate life was how to make complex ideas easy to understand.) So I will save you the thought process and tell you right up front: this isn't new stuff. It is old stuff put in the right order. And it is *exactly* the right approach to take with Millennials!

If you want a formal definition, here it is. Positively Outrageous Service:

- Is random and unexpected
- Is out of proportion to the circumstance
- Involves the customer to a high degree
- Results in positive, compelling word of mouth

In short, Positively Outrageous Service is a simple matter of delivering a *wow* to an unsuspecting customer. It's the service story they can't wait to tell.

But here's something interesting: if you look closely, you will notice that the definition of great service is almost identical to the definition of the worst service you ever had. That awful service was also random and unexpected, it was out of proportion to the circumstance, you were highly involved, and it resulted in compelling, although negative, word of mouth. The difference is that customers like to be surprised in a positive way, and that is the power of POS.

"If the salesperson does not follow the principle of involvement, then they have made a commitment to the opposite, which is failure." —Fred Vang

---

A Taste of Something New

Her name was Anna. I didn't know her last name, but it had to be Italian. Anna was the queen of Little Mike's Ice House on Zarzamora Street in San Antonio, located close to the produce market, in a not-so-nice neighborhood. (If you don't know Texas-speak, *ice house* roughly translates to convenience store. But Little Mike's wasn't only a convenience store; it was a restaurant—a restaurant with no menu, in the least likely location you could imagine.)

What made it special was that Anna served whatever Italian delight her husband, Little Mike, decided he (and therefore you) was hungry for at the moment.

The last time I saw Anna, she was barreling across the concrete-floored eating area with a fork aimed straight at my kisser. The warhead on the missile was a meatball about the size of a tennis ball. I could see the inevitable and thought I stood a good chance of choking to death if Anna's aim held true. Death by meatball—how sweet that death would be! I opened wide as Anna remained on course. Before I knew it, I had somehow kept breathing while clearing my throat of a delicious garlic overdose . . . ahem, ahem. I definitely wanted more.

A few years later (in 1985), we opened a fried chicken franchise and, in response to a competitor, obtained permission from our franchisor to develop chicken tenders as a test product. In a quick-service environment, a share of sales in the 3–6 percent range is considered a success. Our little test product quickly climbed and maintained over 20 percent of sales—a hit, to say the least.

Who was responsible? Anna!

Taking a page from her book, I had small Styrofoam cups filled with white cream gravy. Into each cup I put a hot, fresh, juicy chicken tender. To every customer for the next week I simply said, "Try this." And they did. And it was good.

We were always on the lookout for ways to surprise and delight our customers. For several years, one of our wows came in the form of white chocolate macadamia nut cookies. You couldn't buy them because they weren't on the menu. We didn't know ourselves what days we would serve them; it just happened. And if you were at the right place at the right time, a hot, fresh, gooey cookie would appear on your plate (or in your to-go bag). We spent a few bucks on surprises . . . and we earned additional sales and tons of positive, compelling word of mouth.

Something Unexpected

We were driving around Loop 635 in Dallas one hot summer afternoon when Buns pointed out a large sign that said Boot City.

"Take the next exit," said the former brunette. "You need a new pair of dress boots."

"It's too hot for shopping."

"It will be cool inside," she said with finality.

I know better than to argue; we pulled into the lot. The heat rising off the asphalt only made the already scorching day hotter. That whiff of cool air that greeted me when opening the door was a good sign, but inside there was a better sign: a friendly smile.

"Hey! How are y'all? What can I do for you?" the salesman asked.

"Just looking." I meant it.

"We have just about any boot you could want in almost any size. Where would you like to start?"

"I'm really not thinking boots. I'm thinking beer. Beer so cold you could . . . "

Right then, Mr. Happy interrupted me, saying, "Check out these boots. I'll be right back."

In a few minutes, I was holding a cold can of beer! Where it came from, I do not know. . . . I bought the boots.

Here's another example. When it comes to selling cars, Fred Vang is the master. He is also pretty good at mixing fresh fruit drinks. (Only Fred would think to combine selling cars and mixing fruit drinks! But he understands the value of a little surprise.)

In the early days, Fred worked at a dealership across the street from a health food store that featured a juice bar. Fred, being Fred, made friends with the management and was even allowed to mix his own orange or carrot juice drinks.

Whenever it seemed natural, Fred would invite his customer to walk across the street for a refreshing drink while they discussed the potential purchase. Fred would slip behind the counter, offer fresh orange or carrot juice, and pull up a stool to continue the conversation. A small idea? Not when you consider that at the dealership, the average closing rate was 20 to 25 percent while Fred at the juice bar closed 75 percent or more.

Fred has a great philosophy: stop wondering why you have no customers. Your customers are somewhere. Go out. Find them. They have problems you can solve. Extend a hand. Offer a solution. Attract them to you.

When Fred had no customers coming into the store, he would jump in his car and cruise the freeway in search of someone who had a flat or a breakdown. He would get help or bring them gas, and they would do everything they could to pay him for the rescue. But Fred would never take money; instead, he would give them his card and say, "If you are ever in need of a new car or know anyone who is, I would love to help!"

A Little Something Extra

Here is a *huge* point: only competent organizations will practice Positively Outrageous Service. They recognize that POS creates positive, compelling word-of-mouth marketing—at no additional cost! (Put that in your marketing budget!)

Of course we could *talk* about Positively Outrageous Service all day long. Or I could show you what it looks like. You'd rather see it in action? I thought so. Here are five more examples.

Story 5

I don't know why I asked Christy McNeill for more stories of Positively Outrageous Service at Southwest Airlines. I have enough SWA stories to last a lifetime. I had difficulty choosing the best story from the pile, so I closed my eyes and stabbed a finger at the printed pages, and this is what came up:

> On July 3rd, we flew to Columbus to visit family, and it just so happened it was also our daughter Alyssa's 7th birthday. She was not happy about having to spend her day on a plane, so in a desperate attempt to make the best out of it, we tried to jazz it up by having her wear a "Birthday Princess" pin. Grudgingly, she wore her pin for the day, and the flight attendants on the second leg of our trip from Las Vegas to Columbus took notice of it.
>
> Toward the end of the flight, one of the attendants . . . announced on the P.A. that it was her birthday and then brought out a homemade "birthday cake"—a roll of toilet paper with stir sticks sticking out of the top like candles, decorated with drawings of balloons and the signatures of the flight crew!
>
> They had the whole plane of passengers light their call lights (her candles) and sing Happy Birthday to her. Once they were finished singing, Aly pretended to blow out the candles while everyone turned their lights off. The attendants then presented her with a birthday package of flight snacks and warm smiles. Aly was ECSTATIC! All smiles, she claimed it was the best birthday ever.

We can assume this happy customer was a Millennial because not only did she write Southwest Airlines this wonderful testimonial letter, she posted it, complete with pictures, on Facebook! This is what customers do: they share their experiences, good and bad.

Story 4

It was a special evening. (But then, any time spent with the Brocks, our long-time friends, is special.) We were at the River's Edge, a Tuscan Grille on the banks of the beautiful Guadalupe River in our hometown of Kerrville, Texas. We were completely enjoying ourselves, except for the mini—wine crisis we were experiencing.

Red or white, sweet or dry, not one of us was certain of our pick from the extensive wine list. Our server, a movie star–quality brunette, quietly excused herself, leaving us to our deliberations. Or so we thought.

Soon she returned to our table carrying a tray with several open bottles of wine. "We are going to have ourselves a tasting," she announced. She poured a taste in one glass and passed it to one of the ladies. "This is the one I've picked for you. It's dry but not too dry. Do you like it?" She poured another taste. "I think this one will be perfect with your dinner choice. What do you think?"

We were pleasantly surprised, had a chance to participate, and were made to feel special by the attention and resourcefulness of our server. And she was rewarded, very well I might add, for her Positively Outrageous Service!

Story 3
A guest who used to stay at the Hampton Inn property where Carla Karol had previously worked checked in at a new location and was pleasantly surprised to see her there. Carla, a Guest Services Manager, remembered his name and greeted him with her warm smile. As he was making his way to his room, she called housekeeping to have wine glasses delivered to his room. Why? Because she remembered this was his preference at the other hotel.

He was stunned. Not only did she remember his name, but she remembered the "one little thing" that really mattered to him—wine glasses.

Story 2
If you want great service, any table will do, but when Buns and I are in our favorite restaurant in New Orleans, we know to ask for a table commanded by Jim McDaniel.

Now how do you suppose I remember the name of a server in a restaurant that we visit only a couple of times a year? It's simple. He gave us his card. Yep! A server with a business card. Now that's what I call a Service Natural.

Story 1

This one comes from my friend Roy Smith, in his own words:

> My wife and I were at the Magnolia Cafe in Austin one Sunday morning and were shown to the back patio. We watched as the hostess spoke to another woman eating her breakfast at a side table. She promptly hopped up and came over to wait on us.
>
> We were in no particular hurry, so I said, "Please, finish your breakfast." She smiled and said, "All in good time, sir. All in good time." She very pleasantly took our drink order and continued to provide great (and very funny—matching me smart-ass remark for smart-ass remark) service for the next hour. I'm not sure she ever actually finished her own breakfast!
>
> She made our family morning together so light-hearted and enjoyable, I gladly tipped her $20 on a $24 ticket and have been mentioning the place to friends ever since. She was Positively Outrageous Service personified.

The common thread in all these stories is the value of a little something extra. Positively Outrageous Service works because it has an element of a delightful surprise. It's unexpected, it's darned personal, and it's over the top, bigger than the customers would have imagined. That's what makes it effective. And memorable.

And by the way, this law of selling applies equally across the generations. Everyone responds to a pleasant surprise!

"There are certain laws that you can't fight or you will lose every time. There is the Law of Gravity, the Laws of Motion and Momentum . . . and these laws especially apply to selling. If you fight the laws, the laws win. But if you go with the law rather than against it . . . you will win every time."
—Fred Vang

Treat Me Right When Things Go Wrong

Fred says customers aren't listening because they haven't learned they can trust you. One of the best ways to earn the right to be trusted is to do the right thing when things go wrong. A great salesperson almost begs for an opportunity to make-up for a screw-up.

Customer complaints are part of the game. Sometimes the customer is right, sometimes not—but then the customer is always right, right? If you are sure you were right, explain yourself, apologize for the misunderstanding, and move on. Most people with a complaint are only looking for a reasonable explanation. What counts here, whether wrong or right, is that an apology is in order, if not for the deed itself, certainly for not being clear.

If you were wrong, it is best to go back to the FUSE process from chapter 3:

1. **Friend** the customer with an apology.

2. **Uncover** the exact nature of the problem at hand. Ask questions to be sure you understand the real problem.

3. **Solve** the problem . . . completely! Here is where our process takes a bit of a turn. In this step, let the customer tell you how the issue should be resolved. Fair and friendly conflict resolution demands that emotions stay out of the picture. Be willing to let the customer determine the definition of fair.

4. **Execute** your agreement and expand the emotion of the moment. After you have apologized and resolved the issue, do something extra, something you did not have to do. Something that goes above and beyond, that will make them talk. Something random and unexpected, out of proportion to the circumstance, something that highly involves the customer, that becomes the service story they just can't wait to tell. Does that sound familiar? You got it! Give them a little Positively Outrageous Service!

You should have a policy that says, "We do whatever it takes to make things right when things go wrong."

> *The cheapest and easiest way to settle a complaint is to ask the customer what would make him happy.*

Here is the surprising result. In response to that question, almost every time, they will ask you for less than you would have settled for after negotiating. Did you get that?

Here is an even bigger surprise. When you ask a customer what you can do to make things right, the majority will ask for nothing more than your apology as well as your promise the situation will not be repeated.

"Every salesperson does the same 'big' thing. It's the little things that allow you to 'wiggle into your customer's heart.'"
—Fred Vang

Make Me Laugh

As I've noted previously, Southwest Airlines is a great example of a company that consistently, efficiently delivers great customer service. They concentrate on what customers value most: fast seating and quick turn-arounds, not assigned seating. And they have maintained their two-bags-checked-free policy while others are collecting fees for that service. With Southwest Airlines, you get more, but you don't pay more.

And maybe the best part is their habit of hiring flight attendants and other employees who bring along their personality at no additional charge. Just about anyone who has ever flown Southwest comes home with a funny story. On a flight from San Antonio to Dallas Love Field Airport, I heard this classic SWA announcement:

> Ladies and gentlemen, we'll be landing at gate 2. The gate agent meeting the flight will have connecting information. But we'll make it easy; your gate is in another terminal. If this is your final destination, there is no need to worry about your baggage. It's not on this flight.

Delivering great service is serious business, but it doesn't always have to be *serious*. You can get the same result with a little friendly humor—maybe better.

Now you know . . . . customers like to be "loved on." In the next chapter, you'll learn how to build, train, and retain a team that will deliver the lovin'!

CHAPTER 8

"Train Me, but Don't Constrain Me"

Among the many challenges facing anyone in the business of marketing products or services, two stand out: (1) you have a workforce that is multigenerational, and (2) your new customers, the Millennials, are a different breed, as you've learned from this book. This translates to two major concerns that are essentially two sides of the same coin. The first is helping your salespeople who are of a different generation learn how to be effective with Millennials; the second is hiring and training Millennials to be excellent sales professionals.

For the first, you need to help older generations understand how the much younger customers think and behave. I sincerely hope that all you have learned so far in this book has given you a good start on that. For the second, this chapter will give you some ideas. You may have to rethink a few things, because as you know by now, these Millennials see the world a little differently.

You've met Fred Vang, automotive consultant and natural practitioner of Positively Outrageous Service, in earlier chapters. One day, he called to tell me about a friend of his who runs a small business. Fred says his friend always gives great customer service but for some reason has not been able to grow his business into profitability.

For a business to support itself, it must grow beyond the owner's ability to single-handedly hold down the fort. He needs a few employees, and that is the problem—employees. According to

Fred's friend, not only is it hard to find good help, it is flat-out impossible.

The morning of his call to me, Fred had visited his friend's business and was thoroughly miffed when he was totally ignored for the first few minutes. He should not have been surprised. The single clerk on duty was wearing a t-shirt with "Don't interrupt me while I'm ignoring you" emblazoned on the front.

"How can anyone expect good service from someone with an attitude like that?" Fred sputtered.

My sympathy was limited. You *can* find good help. You just have to know where to look, know what to look for, make an offer that winners find attractive (it is not all about money), never stop hiring, and here is the big one: Be clear in your standards and never settle for less!

One of our customers sums this up nicely: "When you walk in the door, you feel like you are in a happy place."

Creating a "happy place" is not a matter of letting the inmates run the asylum. Fred's friend should have never allowed Mr. Don't Interrupt Me or his offensive t-shirt through the door! Creating a happy place is not about lowering standards. It is about having high standards and being proud of it. People want to be part of organizations held in high esteem by their customers. And high standards leave more room for fun.

One huge truth explains why people buy from one salesperson—or one company—but not from another, even though the product and deal may be identical.

People like to buy from people they like.

And who do they like? People who like them and who are like them. People want to buy from people who look and behave like they do.

Remember, the new Millennial consumer is a bit different from the average Boomer consumer. Boomers are more interested in establishing a relationship. The Millennials are more likely to have done their research prior to making the purchase. They will be ready to bargain and go somewhere else if not satisfied with the deal. So you need to make sure your sales force is up to the challenge. All this is easier if at least some of the salespeople are Millennials themselves.

Meet the New Employee

We have heard anecdotal evidence that when you hire a Millennial, you get Mom and Dad as part of the deal. A common story involves the Millennial job applicant texting during the interview, asking Mom or Dad for advice in negotiating a starting salary. In a variation on this theme—believe it or not!—Mom actually *shows up* and wants to participate in the interview. (And by the way, if you are stupid enough to hire that candidate, this book isn't going to help.)

What we can say for certain is that many Millennials get a late start in the world of work. Said one Gen X theater manager when I visited his Chattanooga location, "They come in here at eighteen and have never had a job! Can you imagine that? Eighteen! First job! You ask them to clean the restrooms, and they just look at you as if to say, 'You can't be serious.' They haven't got a clue about how things get done."

Here's another perspective, from another industry.

Manuel Garcia appears as laid back as Albuquerque, the city he now calls home. Albuquerque is also home to Sitel, Inc., and its five hundred customer service representative employees, representing three Fortune 500 companies. Finding the right people to interact with the respective clients' customers is complicated. When I asked him via phone about the differences among Millennials, Gen X, and Boomers, Garcia says his experience is that Gen X is a bridge between Millennials and Boomer but a bit closer to the Boomer:

> Gen X and Boomers are similar in that we grew up with a feeling that you had to earn your way. We work to give our children everything so they won't have to struggle as much as we did. Then they [Millennials] show up in the workplace and they have high expectations, like working the best schedule. They want Monday through Friday, nine to five. They put social life first and work second.

He goes on to say that a Millennial expects pep talks while Gen X says, "Just tell me what needs to be done and I will do it." On the other hand, Millennials expect to be trained—as long as it is relevant to what they are doing right now.

Here is where we throw the flag up and say, "Don't bucket!" The older generations are famous for retelling stories that start out "When I was your age . . . " While it is true that most in my generation worked their way through college, the younger generations have been coddled by Mom, Dad (if there is one), and a school system that insists every child emerge as a winner, so how could they not feel entitled? When we parents lower our expectations, we are guilty of teaching entitlement. I guarantee that it will come back to bite us in the butt.

What does this mean to you as a boss or a leader? It means that, chances are, you are dealing with a highly educated but socially unskilled workforce. Where will your future employees learn to clean up after themselves? Where will they learn that flip flops and a tank top are not a smart choice to wear to an interview? Where will they learn that an eight o'clock start means eight o'clock, not "whenever"?

Here is an anecdote that I know is true because it happened to me!

We were hiring for our new restaurant when a young man stopped to request an application. Through the open door, we were able to see someone waiting in the car. We were about to find out exactly who that person was.

The young man completed the application in neatly printed letters and placed it on our manager's desk. He was well spoken, neatly dressed, and clean-cut, if you discounted the large blue smear of a gang tattoo on the back of one hand—something not okay in our small, conservative retirement town. Our manager told the young man that he had a job . . . as soon as he removed the tattoo.

The young man left, only to be replaced in a matter of seconds by the person we'd spotted waiting in the car. It was Dad. Dad told us, in no uncertain terms, that we were discriminating and would be hearing from his attorney, yadda, yadda, yadda. (We didn't flinch.)

Two weeks later, the young man reappeared, again neatly dressed and mannerly, only this time something was missing.

He got the job.

Good stories sometimes have more than one ending, which is the case with this story. After a week's employment, our young friend stopped in about an hour ahead of his shift to pick up his paycheck. Again, we could see the silhouette of his dad waiting in the car. As the son climbed into the SUV, his dad stepped out.

Uh oh! We braced for the coming onslaught of a still-angry parent.

"A few weeks ago, you refused to hire my son over a tattoo," he said, "and I promised you would be hearing from me and my attorney. Well, today, you just get me." We noticed a mood shift, as he seemed to relax, then added, "Thank you. I don't know why your refusal to hire him set me off. I had been trying for months to get him to have the &^%$ thing removed, and you finally got through to him!"

Understand the New Values

Many Millennials don't conform to the older generations' expectations of a salesperson. I say different can be good, as long as you do not compromise your hiring standards. When hiring, choose applicants who will mirror what your customers wear, reflect your customers' language habits, and ably engage the customers with an outgoing personality.

You want skilled Millennials on your sales team. But first you have to find them, and that means you have to understand their attitudes toward work.

Meaningful Work

Millennials just want to earn a good living while doing work that matters, or so the pundits say. Well, duh! Who doesn't want to earn a good living? And who would prefer to do meaningless work for marginally more pay? If I paid you well to dig big holes and then fill them, how long would it take for you or any average human being to say, "Hey! As long as I am going to be here anyway, would you like me to build something?"

Art happens when the work and the worker connect.

Everybody wants to earn a good living doing work that matters, because if you show me that my time doesn't matter, I start to think that maybe *I* don't matter. What is a boss to do?

If you want to motivate someone, connect him directly to his work. Have him sign his work, and then sit back to marvel as quality steadily improves.

Opportunities to Collaborate

Most Millennials love being part of a team. I can think of three reasons why:

1. The school system rewards the team rather than the individual in sports—everyone gets a trophy.

2. Technology supports online team play (think of video games).

3. Millennials have never lived in a time when the United States was as not at war. The military (the ultimate promoters of teamwork) has left us with a generation, maybe two, that knows how to collaborate to solve problems in fluid conditions.

As employees—and again, we want to avoid bucketing—Millennials are not wallflowers. They want to be part of the action. They don't want to observe, they want to participate, and they want their views to carry weight.

Here is something to consider: is it because of this generation's love of diversity that they invite everyone to play, or is it because everyone gets to play that they appreciate diversity? Very interesting!

In 1965, fat girls did not become cheerleaders, pregnant girls did not marry wearing white, and nearsighted boys weren't going to be cool even if they could dance . . . which they could not. In most cities, black kids did not hang with white kids, poor kids did not hang with rich kids, and Baptist kids did not hang with Catholics or Jews.

It is not that way in the twenty-first century. If you are a Millennial, none of the previous labels rise to the level of attention. And that is an ideal situation for leaders smart enough to harness the everybody-is-welcome-to-play power of Millennial teams.

Fun

All work and no . . . the next word is *play*, p-l-a-y. Many Boomers even have difficulty pronouncing the word in a work environment. It is, after all, a *work* environment! (Most Millennials say the older generations have a better work ethic . . . and they do!) But watch any high-performance team for a full day, and you will discover the value of humor. This is particularly true when the work environment is a little stressful. Millennials expect work to be punctuated at least occasionally with humor and fun.

Freedom of Choice

While a Traditional would accept almost any order as long as it came through the proverbial chain of command, Boomers and Gen X might hesitate but comply. But Millennials will balk at doing things "the way we've always done it" because they want freedom of choice in everything. They may not balk at the assignment itself but instead may challenge the methodology.

This quirkiness over process goes hand in hand with their desire to control their work life in order to balance it against their home life. In an odd way, this is similar to the Boomers, who let life click away, one time-clock punch after the other. The only difference is the unit of measurement: Boomers' time put in versus

Millennials' results achieved. Think about that for thirty seconds, and tell me which works in favor of the boss.

Why do you suppose Millennials are concerned about freedom and flexibility? They grew up with higher degrees of parental trust. More than likely, their parents worked. Many were responsible for their own after-school care. Latchkey kids were all too common.

In 1950, if a teenage girl wanted to use the telephone, she would have to ask permission. Most homes in that era had party lines, and telephone usage was reserved for necessity, not frivolities. By 1965, there was a good chance she had her own telephone, probably a Princess model, and could use it as long as she adhered to the tight usage restrictions. Today, she doesn't ask for permission, has few rules regarding phone use, and rarely puts it down between text messages. It's not a land-locked telephone; it's a cell phone that goes everywhere she goes.

And you expect this person to follow your stupid rules to the letter? I think not.

What Hasn't Changed

I don't mean to suggest that your new workforce will consist entirely of alien creatures you can't possibly understand. In fact, right here is exactly where generational characteristics start to blend. Millennials need lots of feedback. Who doesn't? Millennials want a clearly defined career path. They want to be trained so they won't look stupid on the job. They want flexibility when personal events conflict with their work schedule. Who doesn't?

The one positive result in establishing Millennial generational characteristics is this: when we pay attention to their characteristics, we reexamine our management and leadership style, which ultimately brings us full circle: *all* human beings want to feel good, want to do good work and be recognized for it, and actually are pretty good people. This is not rocket science!

As important as the differences between generations may be, it is best to use your knowledge of those differences only as a template.

When dealing with individuals, forget for the moment about generations, and concentrate instead on individuals.

So, if you are the boss, what should you do? Stop being a boss. Instead, be a leader. In a nutshell, this means you will do the following: hire great people, train them to fulfill your vision, get out of the way, and finally, say thank you for a job well done.

One last piece of advice: be yourself, and act your generation. Of the living generations, none is more put off by phoniness than Millennials. Millennials respect authenticity, so chill, dude! (LOL)

Hire Great People

Before you even think about sales technique, you have to consider who is going to do the selling; just any warm body won't do. The first job of a leader is to assemble a team of winners!

The problem is that so few people find their way to such an idyllic match. It's certainly true in sales. There are plenty of folks who are good at sales and an even larger group who can't stand the thought of sales. It would make sense to hire and train only the people who like to sell, want to sell, and at least have the potential for getting good at it.

It would make sense. But we don't.

Imagine that you have a pair of glasses that allow you to see an applicant's potential for giving great customer service. If you used those glasses to sort applicants into three groups, about 15 percent would fall into the lowest category, which we call Service Impossibles. These are people who, no matter how much incentive, feedback, negative consequences, or training you provide, are simply not going to give great customer service. You will be fortunate if they don't send your customers running to the competition.

For every person there is a perfect job, and for every job there is a perfect person.

Think of the person in your work group most likely to not show up for a busy shift. Got a picture? That's the one we are talking about. Here is what to do: fire him today!

The middle group, the Service Possibles, represent more than our biggest group at 70 percent; they represent our biggest challenge as well as our biggest opportunity. These are the fence sitters who can go either way. Because their performance is only satisfactory, they receive the least attention. They're not bad enough for discipline, but not good enough for praise. The success or failure of the Service Possibles is determined by one thing and one thing only: leadership.

Given proper training and tools, and the example of an inspired leader, Service Possibles can turn in a respectable performance. Unfortunately, that seldom happens because many managers are *themselves* Service Possibles who have either received insufficient training, work with insufficient tools, or have an appalling lack of leadership skills.

Service Naturals make up the remaining 15 percent. These are the people who will deliver great customer service no matter what. Without training, tools, or leadership, Service Naturals will bust their chops to give the customer a great experience. Why? Because that is what Service Naturals do. It is who they are. It is their nature.

You can find them. You can hire them. How do we know? Because somebody already has!

Most of the problems managers face are people problems that stem from a mismatch between the requirements of the job and the ability of the employee to meet those requirements. The problem is exacerbated when dealing with Millennials due to their short attention span and notorious tendency to switch jobs. One sometimes-forgotten reason Millennials are wont to play the employment version of musical chairs is that so many of them are underemployed. Another counter to the received wisdom on Millennials and employment is that people don't leave jobs they love, and they love jobs where they are loved.

Hire for Attitude

It may be tempting to look for technical skill sets, but the smart operator hires for attitude and trains for skills. Interpersonal skills are not easily learned in a corporate setting, but technical skills are. (Millennials may not have enough work experience to easily predict on-the-job performance, but what they lack in work experience may be offset by their digitally acquired social skills.) If you hire someone with incredible skills and he ticks off your customers, just how far ahead do you think you are?

You might be surprised that a Service Natural is only slightly more sociable than average. If you think about it, would you want to be served by someone who was so busy talking that taking your order was only an afterthought? You also might be thinking that high energy would be important. No. What is important is constant attention, a willingness to follow the rules, and the ability to be flexible without getting walked on.

Ask Strong Questions

Hiring a Millennial could get dicey because many have relatively little work experience. If you evaluate them by traditional standards, you risk missing true talent.

To interview Millennials properly, you should focus your questions on intangible yet valuable experiences. To uncover a talent for networking, ask about their use of social media. You may discover that they use social media to greater purpose than simple chat. Pose a few simple problems, and watch for signs of resourcefulness, imagination, and perseverance.

These questions are only four of the more than one hundred behavioral questions generated by The McQuaig Job Survey® represented by Bill Wagner of Accord Management Systems. We use these four questions to make a quick determination about whether there is any need to schedule a second interview. If it is immediately obvious that the individual doesn't fit, there is no need to spend additional time or resources. If the applicant seems to fit, then make the decision to proceed with the hiring process.

Service Naturals will deliver the best service possible, no matter what . . . It's their nature.

1. **Tell me about a time when you were involved in a competition.** (Listen for a dominant or accepting response; is the response appropriately balanced?)

2. **Tell me your thoughts about how employees should interact with customers.** (Listen for a sociable or analytical response; Service Naturals will be friendly but remain focused on business.)

3. **Work environments can be relaxed or rushed. Which do you prefer? Why?** (Listen for a relaxed or driving response; will this person respond well in busy periods?)

4. **What are your thoughts about following rules?** (Listen for a compliant or independent response; Service Naturals know which rules should be challenged and which rules must be followed exactly.)

In an economy of high unemployment, labor is a buyer's market. That means you'll be able to choose from more applicants for jobs requiring minimal skills. But for jobs requiring special training, the situation is reversed. In that case, you will have to get better at being the employer of choice. And when you identify a Service Natural, hire him!

Train Your People

The Millennials like to learn, and they expect on-the-job training. But be warned that traditional, stand-up, teacher-centric training may not work. As a matter of fact, it will *definitely* not work, particularly for Millennials. For training to work, you must satisfy two conditions. First, the trainee must see immediate application. Second, the training must involve spaced repetition. An additional requirement with Millennials is that the training must be outcome driven.

Our son, who is a late Gen X, provided the perfect example of how the Millennial views training. One early morning, I was driving him to high school and, being a parent, I asked how he had done on a test I had helped him study for.

"Terrible, Dad."

"Terrible? How could you have done terrible? When we worked on it together, you knew every answer perfectly. How could you possibly have done terrible?" I fired off a few questions I remembered from our study session, and he was right. He was terrible. I started to get angry, but he beat me to the punch.

"Dad, I'll never use that information again. I don't care about it. I just flushed it!"

As a former corporate trainer, one of the first things I learned was that learning requires spaced repetition of the material. Once a trainer, always a trainer! While searching for an online training platform for one of my clients, I discovered BrainX.com and agree with their recommended guidelines:

- Survey your training needs, and break them into bites of twenty minutes, preferably less, never more.
- Prepare a lesson in a format that can be self-administered, and make it available via web or smartphone.
- Use spaced repetition.

After they studied how learning occurs, BrainX.com taught us that the brain waits for sleep before it transfers fresh information into long-term memory. It's simple! And that's why training in most corporate settings is ineffective and a waste of time and money. Old school is to present the information and test immediately—*before* the brain has transferred anything into long-term memory, where it can be retrieved for use when needed.

It certainly makes good sense to train Millennials on computers or even iPhones. That's their stomping ground, so to speak.

Know the Good and Bad News About Performance

Today's worker has a limited attention span. Tomorrow's worker will have even less.

What do you do with a worker who has the attention span of a gnat? (I just had this image of a gnat writing a business book and asking, "What do you do with a worker who has the attention span of a Millennial?") The answer is the same in either case. You load up those neurons with additional input, and you give them more to do.

Here is what will be different with Millennials. They require short-term, measurable goals with tons of feedback in small increments of time. They can and will perform, but only if they are given proper feedback and appreciation for a job well done.

The news doesn't get better; it gets worse. When asked about the tenure of their workforce, the HR director of one big company replied, "The Boomers are good for about ten years, then it is up or out. Gen X is good for four, maybe five years. As for Millennials, we measure their tenure in months and we are averaging about eighteen, maybe less." Despite record unemployment, turnover is particularly high in entry-level jobs. Quick-service restaurants (fast food) frequently experience a turnover rate in excess of 300 percent. Why? Because workers know they can get another job in an instant. In many markets, employers avoid asking why an applicant left their previous job . . . They just don't want to know!

Some Millennials regard having a job as a right that falls under the government's responsibility to provide. And they have the previously mentioned definitions of what makes a good job: flexible hours and policies, respect, variety, and opportunity for further training and growth. They have little or no tolerance for red tape, stupid rules, or dress codes. And since they have mastered the transition of media in one place to media anyplace, they wonder why should you care where the work was done or even how many hours it took, as long as it gets done?

The good news is how hard they work.

Understand Millennial Attitudes and Beliefs

For employers, then, the trick is to understand these young workers and get inside their heads. It doesn't make sense to try to train people to go against their natural inclinations when you can turn those inclinations into positives. So first of all, get to know them.

You may be interested in a research project we created to look deeper into the collective psyche of Millennials with an ongoing survey of their attitudes and beliefs. We produced two identical surveys, one for respondents born prior to 1973 and another for those born after (Millennials).

We constructed our survey as a ranking between two opposites and asked the respondents to choose between the two extremes using a scale of zero to ten (see figure 10, page 105). Rather than dig into scores and insignificant statistics, let's look at broad points of difference. No survey could make a statement such as "One group is 12.55 percent more likely to [fill in the blank]" and be meaningful. Instead, let's explore the *relative* differences first. Here are the choices by category and a few comments before we show the survey scores.

1. **Execution:** Do things right versus Do the right things. Boomers know that doing the right thing well beats doing the wrong thing perfectly. When we asked which was more important, doing things right or doing the right thing, Millennials as a group opted for doing things right.

2. **Competition:** Go get the business versus Let customers come to you. Boomers are still the hunter-gatherers. In terms of the cohort and not individuals, Millennials are slightly less aggressive when it comes to seeking business.

3. **Innovation:** The old way is proven versus If you have a new idea, try it. Innovation is only marginally less important to our sample of Millennials.

4. **Value:** Customers want low prices versus Customers will pay a premium for quality. Surprise! The Millennials we surveyed were more likely to pay for premium product and service, but you have to focus on the benefits rather than the features.

5. **Casualness:** Uniforms required versus Dress comfortably.Even comfortable dress can be regarded differently depending on the generation—for example, blue jeans casual versus Dockers casual!

6. **Integrity:** Business is business versus Make moral decisions. Both cohorts agree on moral decisions.

7. **Work ethic/lifestyle:** Work comes first versus Take care of yourself first. Surprise! Regarding work attitudes, our surveys show little difference between the two groups.

8. **Hiring:** Okay to hire family and friends versus Not okay to hire family and friends. What surprised us was Millennials' answer to the question of whether it was a good idea to hire two or more people from the same group or family. Despite the perception that Millennials are too close with their friends and family, their answer was no!

9. **Reward/recognition:** Individual performance is rewarded versus We reward teamwork. Millennials have a bias toward teamwork and team reward.

10. **Freedom:** We demand punctuality versus As long as the job gets done, work hours won't be an issue. One big and quite expected point of difference is that Millennials will fight for their time off and freedom from punching a time clock. But when working on a time-crunched project, they will work hard to get it done. Expect them to ask for time off in return. Millennials expect a little flexibility.

11. **Compensation:** I prefer higher salary/lower benefits versus I prefer lower salary/higher benefits. Millennials prefer the cash!

12. **Communication:** Quick to anger versus Speak with reason. We almost matched again!

13. **Risk:** Screw-ups are punished versus Intelligent risk is encouraged. Look who's not much for risk . . . the Millennials!

14. **Authority:** Approval is required for decisions versus Employees are empowered to make customer-centric decisions. Millennials highly value freedom to do things their way and with little supervision. (Freedom is one of this generation's defining character traits.)

15. **Customer complaint resolution policy:** Delights customers versus Frustrates customers. Another close match!

16. **Politics:** We don't tolerate employee gossip at all versus Gossip is interesting. A surprising difference here! Is this the result of social media? The Millennials tend to be more accepting of office gossip. Maybe reality TV shows have helped glamorize this bad habit, or maybe it's due to all that Twittering!

17. **Advancement:** Entitled versus Earned; Tenure trumps merit versus Merit trumps tenure. Now it's the Boomers' turn to a little entitlement!

18. **Wellness:** On site, any time, company provided versus That's not the company's responsibility. Millennials call for more flexibility.

19. **Training:** Minimal versus Extensive. Both cohorts agree on the amount of training, but notice how their opinions differ in the next score.

20. **Training delivery:** Instructor led versus Learner controlled. Millennials definitely want to be in control.

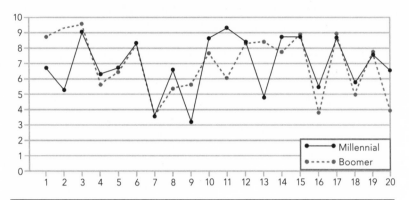

Figure 10: Culture calculator.

Measure Success

You want to know how things are going, but how do you measure effectiveness? You may already have some performance metrics that you've been using for years. Here's the bad news: they may not work all that well with Millennials.

The Millennials present a measuring problem. They work best with lots and lots of feedback—instant feedback, if possible. So measure, measure, measure, but be careful! Measuring the wrong thing can be worse than not measuring at all.

There are two big problems with sales and service metrics, and a few small ones. Most companies do not do metrics, or if they do, they often measure the wrong things (these are the big problems). Then, if companies get lucky enough to get the right numbers, those data either are received too late, or we ignore them. Pretty positive, huh?

The biggest problems come when sales metrics are linked to compensation. You have heard the old saying, "What you inspect, people respect." Or an even better saying is, "You get more of what you measure." If you measure speed of service, what do you get? Fast service. But could you serve so fast that customers didn't have time to continue to buy and sales per customer go down? It's those darned unintended consequences!

Could a measure of sales per transaction result in customers feeling pressured? The most common sales performance measurement is customer satisfaction. Well, has anyone ever gone to the bank and deposited customer satisfaction?

The best performance metrics include both individual and team scores. They should be constantly visible, and the participants should have the responsibility of measuring their own performance.

We talk so much about customer service that we overlook the fact that, by nature, most service positions are in fact *sales* positions, albeit positions in which selling is but an afterthought, other than the occasional posting of sales per transaction or sales per employee. Even then, it is unlikely that the employee involved will ever see or benefit from the information unless the numbers are used for a sales contest.

Recognize the Benefits

If we are on target with our prediction, it looks like managing Millennial team members is going to be tough. (Do you think managing Gen X was not a problem? Well, Gen X were and still are a problem! And Boomers? Were they anywhere near perfect? Not even. Just ask a Traditional!) The real problem is that too few managers in any generation were smart enough to deliver the feedback, the clear career path, and the matrix training that all generations would have benefited from.

What's the difference? Millennials are probably going to demand all of these things—feedback, career path, and matrix training—and if they get them, everybody wins!

If you have read this far, chances are you are not a Millennial. No, chances are you're a Boomer or Gen X, and you are amazed, amused, and somewhat mystified by those alien creatures, the Millennials.

From many perspectives, it would have been fair to label them Gen Y Not. Why not give workers frequent feedback? Why not train them closer to the time when they will need the information? Why not give them more freedom as to when and how they complete a task, as long as it is completed on time and done correctly? And why should we be offended by customers who want us to sell, serve, and market invisibly?

Tell me why Millennials should show loyalty to Generation Because-I-Said-So! Why?

We have forever changed our world with technology—some for the better, some for the worse. With a little understanding and a lot of foresight, the customer's experience will only get better—for all. And why not?

PART THREE
The Crystal Ball

CHAPTER 9

What's Next?

In the 1970s, it seemed as though you couldn't hold a convention unless there was a futurist on the program. These days you don't see many futurists, and it makes you wonder: if they were so darned smart, why didn't they predict that by 2011, most would be unemployed?

I remember attending a conference in 1972 where the futurist du jour said, "By the year 2000, the biggest problem in America will be what to do with our spare time. Thanks to the personal computer, Americans will finish their work by Wednesday, possibly as late as Thursday, and then they will be looking for something to do."

May I see a show of hands of all those who experienced a problem finding something to do? I thought so. Computers have not allowed us to finish our work sooner. They allow us to do more work faster! They may be responsible for higher productivity, but spare time? Not even!

The Path to Progress

From where I sit, the world looks a little gloomy. It's as if the earth shook and broke into two huge pieces, creating a chasm we could fairly call the digital divide. On one side stand the huge number of unemployed (as I write, it's 9.2 percent), looking bewildered, surprised to be left behind, and uncertain about how to cross that chasm.[18]

On the other side is the potential future, inhabited by a host of beings created out of silicon and ideas, cobbled together with the intent that these artificially intelligent avatars would make life easier. (They were not designed with the intention that nearly one in ten of our friends and neighbors would be out of work, replaced by computers.)

That aspect of the future, at least, is not really new. My first encounter with my wife was over the phone. She was the PBX operator at the same company where I worked. ("Good afta-noon, A&W International. How may I direct your call?") She began as a switchboard operator for Ohio Bell and quickly became a pro at plugging wires into jacks to complete your call. She could listen to the coins fall into the pay phone and know how much you had deposited. Now there are no switchboards, no PBXs. When they left, so did the jobs.

Think of all the jobs that have disappeared, and you may think, well, that's progress. But consider the jobs that technology is likely to eliminate in the coming years. It may still be progress, but the possibilities are frightening. For Millennials who are too young to remember the historical vibrancy of manufacturing in their towns—whose only image of America as manufacturer comes complete with boarded-up windows—losing jobs to foreign markets may just be part of the excitement of playing globally.

We have to totally rethink our concept of work and who's going to be doing it.

The Future of Employees

You could say the employee of the future is a little different. He has no eyes, but he can look up your record. He has no ears, but he can listen to your complaint. He has no mouth, but he can answer your questions . . . in several languages. He has no heart, but we can fix that. He can be a she. It's up to you.

Of course, we are talking about an avatar gifted with artificial intelligence. We could give the avatar an artificial body to house the artificial intelligence, but why take up space when a whole colony of avatars can live comfortably on your hard drive?

Hello. I'm Sarah and I am a CyberTwin, the most advanced artificial IQ on the planet. I have a human personality, am trained to think through complex tasks, and my advanced brain learns through experience. As I chat with people, I build their profiles, answering questions while responding to each person individually. In fact, most people forget they are interacting with an avatar.

So began the demo of MyCyberTwin, created by Dr. John Zakos and now owned by IBM. The visual was that of an attractive, professionally attired customer service representative who waits patiently on standby until the viewer is ready to cue her formal introduction. While she waits, her eyes blink, humanlike. She slightly shifts her weight from one side to another, like you would in a similar situation. In three words, she looks human. She sounds human, too. And her talents? Remarkable!

During the transaction, your customer relationship management system can pass information to the Twin. Not only is the Twin able to receive, evaluate, and react to incoming data, it can use fuzzy logic to detect and respond to the emotions and personality of the customer. With this customer, it speaks with a sophisticated London accent. Next, a sweet southern drawl.

Online avatars can offer personalized customer support, outbound or inbound client sales, and even entertainment and companionship. Your Twin can browse the Internet with you, evaluate offers, and play games . . . anywhere, including on mobile devices such as the iPhone.

Here is the creepy part: this inanimate speck of silicon can adopt multiple personalities, upload class-specific data, and train itself! A Twin can remember 2,000 points of customer-relevant information and 100 to 150 profile variables.

Speaking of profiles, MyCyberTwin constantly profiles the caller by asking questions to figure out how technically savvy the caller is. The Twin can handle slang, abbreviations, and misspellings; and if it comes across something it has not yet encountered, it will look at all the words in the sentence, weigh them, and make an accurate guess at the meaning.

Before you turn up your nose and discount the idea of being served by a robot, you probably should know that 70 percent of those who interact with MyCyberTwin are happy with the service and a full 95 percent don't notice any difference! That's right—unless told otherwise, up to 95 percent of customers think they are dealing with a human. Even when they know they're dealing with a computer, humans treat MyCyberTwins as humans. To avoid training customers to be rude to "real" humans, these avatars can be trained to detect rudeness and push back appropriately!

And to match the experience exactly to the marketing department's specs, your Twin can be programmed to match the personality of the brand. Imagine that! An avatar so smooth, you can't tell it isn't human. Incredible!

If you could replace a human employee with a computerized avatar, why wouldn't you? Weekly payroll? None. Benefits package? Not necessary. Supervision? Take a break . . . a long one.

Think of all the jobs that could be handled well by this new, exciting, and definitely frightening technology.

But wait, you say. Surely there are some jobs that just can't be filled by a handful of silicon chips. You might be surprised. Note the following, from an article by Richard Conniff in the June 2011 edition of *Smithsonian*:

- The Federal Aviation Administration is already considering new rules and training controllers to adjust to unmanned aircraft in US airspace. Peter Singer, an analyst with the Brookings Institution, says it may be 2012 or 2014, but whatever the date, it is going to happen. The military has been working on cockpit automation for years, first testing the concept in the 1990s in a highly automated F-18. His opinion? "On carrier landings, they always did better than humans."[19]

- Boeing and Airbus jets now take off, land, and brake to a stop without human hands on the control stick. Aviation researchers predict that by 2021, cargo planes will fly without human pilots, and passenger jets will ultimately follow.

- A UPS or FedEx plane might have one human pilot to communicate with air traffic control and three unmanned planes flying in formation behind.

Wow! Pretty amazing—unless you are a pilot and want to make a living flying airplanes!

The Future of Customer Service

I predict . . . many product-smart consumers will demand that the service portion of a product be unbundled from the offer, and (here is the kicker!) they will accept responsibility for their own tech support. This change will be made possible in part by the availability of information and community on the Internet, in addition to products that are more intuitive. In recent years, more products come with a knowledge component built right in (such as plug-and-play installation of computers and their peripherals or television sets that guide you through set-up in multiple languages). Companies that offer service "good enough to pay for" (and you know who you are!) will be the exception in the forced-to-unbundle market.

I predict . . . customization will be the rule rather than the exception. There is no reason in a digital world why any customer should not be offered the ability to customize her purchases. Custom music, custom clothes, custom automobiles, custom just about anything you want. (What are tattoos and piercings other than Millennials customizing themselves?)

I predict . . . labor will become a buyer's market. Jobs lost to technology are not coming back. Period. When businesses cut back on staff, they sometimes make an amazing discovery—the missing staff aren't missed! Employers find that with the help of technology, they can be more profitable without the overhead of the additional employees. I see three reasons why the missing employees are gone forever:

1. Boomers are not retiring on cue. There are too few
    empty slots on the time-card rack to accommodate the
    Millennials entering the labor market and the Gen Xs
    moving up.

2. For many jobs, the competition is global, with work
    requiring only a computer and high-speed Internet
    access.

3. Many service jobs are going to avatars that consum-
    ers say they like as well as or better than humans. They
    work 24/7 and do not require benefit packages, making
    them cheaper than employees.

I predict . . . HR will be the go-to department when the
C-suites go looking for untapped competitive advantage. The companies that can hire, train, and motivate most efficiently will have
a distinct competitive edge.

One last prediction: this morning's email included notifica-
tions from Twitter, Facebook, LinkedIn, and several less public
sites. I haven't got time to deal with so much social media—I have
a life! Like Betamax or VHS, we are going to make choices. Some
sites will lose, some sites will win. Some sites will evolve, but
many of us will begin to suffer social media fatigue if we have not
already.

A Play-by-Play Peek Ahead

Whatever you do, don't blink! The world is changing so quickly
that predictions are little more than play-by-play analysis. But for
what it's worth, here are some things I've been thinking about:

*   Increasingly we will see the boss as a parental figure
    who will have to train employees in matters, such as
    work ethic, that used to be learned at home.

*   Social media will become more diverse, making main-
    taining a presence more challenging. For example,
    LinkedIn has become the leading site for professionals,
    over Facebook.

- Competition for those folks we call Service Naturals may lead to something that resembles certification of the best of the best.

- More and more products will include high knowledge content, reducing the pressure for customer service. Complex equipment will self-diagnose and, in many cases, automatically call for a technician. Voice recognition will continue to improve until a conversation with tech support may be person-to-computer or perhaps computer-to-computer.

Some Things Never Change

Sometimes we get so deep into the weeds looking for the esoteric nuance that we tend to miss the obvious, simple truths. We focus so intently on what is going to be new that we miss those things that are not likely to change.

Human nature is not likely to change in the foreseeable future. The context in which we express our humanness may change, but not our nature. What do we know for absolute certain about human beings?

- We know we like to be right.

- We know we like to be part of something greater than ourselves.

- We know we like to feel good, and we avoid things that make us feel bad.

And all of that is good news for businesses. It means you can continue doing the right things the same way you do now. Thoughtful, compassionate companies can, if they put their minds to it, handle the future and nurture the best of the present. We don't know for sure what is going to happen, but it's going to be a heck of a lot of fun to watch.

PART FOUR

Things You Should Have Learned at Home . . . But Probably Didn't!

CHAPTER 10

As the Saying Goes . . .

"You can't cure stupid." Ronald White, philosopher

"There's your sign." Lawrence the Cable Guy, philosopher

"You might be a redneck if . . ." Jeffrey Foxworthy, philosopher

"There is no dumbass vaccine." James Buffett, poet, philosopher, musician

My first choice for the title of this chapter was "There Is No Dumbass Vaccine." Unfortunately, or maybe fortunately, I couldn't get it past the head office (Buns). Having worked in both hospitality and retail I have seen thousands of individuals with all the potential in the world screw up their lives with dumbass decisions. I don't particularly like using the word dumbass but frankly, it's the best word for the job at hand.

I'd like to gently point out a few of the dumbass things Millennials are inclined to do in the faint hope that they will see themselves heading down a one-way road and turn before it's too late.

"There is no dumbass vaccine," is a line from one of my favorite Jimmy Buffett songs. When he sings that line, it's funny. But when I try to use it, it's awkward, kind of sixth-grade humor. When we were in sixth grade, like most pre-pubescent, snot-nosed kids, we confused scatological humor and crude language with urban, grown-up sophistication. We were wrong but we didn't know it.

Few of us grow completely out of that phase. Instead, it holds us spellbound, captured by an aura of stupidity that often lasts well into adulthood, like the KFC employee arrested for selling marijuana from the drive-thru window. His secret password for customers interested in ganja to go: "I'd like extra biscuits!"

Dumbass! (Sorry! That's about as nice as I can be in describing this moron.)

You may be reading this chapter because you have a dumbass in your life and you want to use this book as a see-I-told-you-so weapon. Well, that is a dumbass thing to do! You aren't going to change them. You'll be lucky to change yourself!

Why Millennials Need Rules

If a generation is defined by values and experiences as anchored by the music and ceremony of its formative years, then the source of those values and experiences matters considerably. The world is changing so rapidly that it is risky to mention current figures in something as lasting as a book. By the time this book is published, only those who are in serious need of a life may remember Miley Cyrus swinging from a wrecking ball or the Bieb and his problems with neighbors and eggs.

The human psyche records and stores values and experiences forever. Tell me the toddler shown on YouTube last week will not remember being taught to rap about hoes and bitches. He will remember . . . forever. He and an entire generation will, till the end of their days, act on the values and experiences anchored in the music and ceremony of their formative years.

You can try to ignore the following facts but that will neither change them nor make them disappear. Millennials drew the short straw in several categories. Shall I name them?

- Millennials are being left with a boatload of national debt that they will be decades paying off, if ever.

- Millennials, especially males, are falling behind in education, particularly in math, science, and reading.

- Millennials have all but divorced marriage and more and more children are growing up in households without a dad, (although there may be a transient 'boyfriend' or two or three.)

- Millennials are leaving the church and learning their morals and ethics on the street or on the Internet.

To sum up: no church, no dad, less mom, inherited debt. As parents, Boomers could have done a whole lot better.

Leading the Under-Class

Isn't this statement true?

The under-class trades minimum skills for minimum wage.

I fully expect that someone who has only read this far has decided to take me to task for even hinting that (a) there is an under-class, and (b) they are different. Well, there is and they are.

Buns and I were sitting in the hot tub talking about a recent article in *Rolling Stone*. I would love to mention that we were up to our naked necks in hot, bubbling water, sipping Pinot Grigio but we weren't. It just paints a better picture when you say hot tub.

The author of the article (not in our hot tub) was encouraging Millennials to fight for guaranteed jobs for those who wanted to work. For others who do not choose to work, a monthly sum sufficient for subsistence would be automatically deposited to their bank account. Also on the list was to "make everything owned by everyone."

The conversation actually started when one of us said, "Minimum wage is for minimum skills. Why are we talking about raising the minimum wage without raising the minimum skills?" followed by an observation that Millennials (not just those who are also included in the under-class) are getting royally screwed by a legacy of Boomer debt. Under greedy Boomer eyes, much of our national wealth has been squandered. And we ask Millennials to trust us?

Education seems to have deteriorated to the point where college has in many cases become the last chance to get a high school education. (I love that line so let me say it again: college has become the last chance to get a high school education.)

The under-class doesn't need a guaranteed subsistence income as suggested in *Rolling Stone*. They need a guaranteed better-than-subsistence opportunity to work their way to the top rather than sit their way to the bottom.

A few years ago we hired a contractor to move a little dirt. The day was hotter than hell and, no surprise, his two helpers failed to show up. So the contractor pulled off his shirt, picked up a shovel, and went to work. He seemed to be humming but when I moved a little closer, I heard instead this little poem being repeated again and again: *Get off of your ass and onto your feet. Get out of the shade and into the heat.*

Rolling Stone apparently does not require its authors to be math majors. (Someone, please, ask where will the money come from?)

The problem is simple. The solutions are not. Mainly because a simple law of nature stands in the way—sitting does not create wealth. Add the complicating fact that the behavior you reward is the behavior you get and you take away all purpose and incentive. Just guess how long civilization could endure.

Having spent a lifetime working with and loving the folks who live at the lower end of the social barrel—the minimum wage earners—I can tell you they don't need socialism that doesn't work. They need capitalism that works. And, they need someone to teach them the rules.

Thanks to technology there are more unbreakable laws popping up nearly every day, just waiting for the next dumbass to come along and break them.

Take for example, selfies of your genitals, an original Millennial dumbass creation. If that isn't a dumbass idea, I don't know what is.

(If I have to explain why selfies of your genitals are a bad idea . . . sheeeesh! You are beyond redemption!)

Have you noticed that some people seem to be lucky? They live in nicer houses. Drive newer cars. They even dress just a little better than the rest of us. Did you ever wonder how that happened to them and not to you?

Well, it's possible they really are lucky but it's more likely that they know something you don't know. They know the Millennial Rules. Millennials did not create these nor were they created just for them. They are just rules of how the real world works.

CHAPTER 11

The Boss as Parent

I fully expect this to be the biggest point of this book.

The successful contemporary leader will be forced to play one more role—the role of Mom or Dad. The boss will in many cases become the source of values and experiences. Basic training—that's what it is—has suddenly become not so basic.

The Millennials are inheriting a world that is flawed to say the least. You would think Boomers would have instilled in Millennials a clear sense of right and wrong. But we haven't. We closed "basic training" before the job was done. Was it because we felt we had already done what we knew to do and there simply was no more?

Yet there is more. And the only way to get there is for the boss to become parent.

I considered putting the Millennial Rules in terms of biblical quotes, perhaps even commandments, but it might have spoiled the message's reception. Instead I chose to list the Millennial Rules that relate most to on-the-job performance in the form of sayings— simple and clear, practical sayings. Use them generously on your Millennials. If you do it lovingly, your efforts will be appreciated even if they are considered corny.

For a starting point, I suggest this:

Pick a Millennial Rule you believe will make the world a better place. Now pick one more Millennial Rule. And another. You start by adopting those two, three, or four Millennial Rules and make them a part of your business life. Say them again and again until your team adopts them out of self-defense.

Then start again.

Think of a saying that a coach or favorite teacher used to drill into you constantly. Maybe at the time it irritated you but today it is part of the way you run your life. Think of something your dad said again and again. You knew he believed it and now you believe it too. That's where to start.

Here are some of my favorite sayings, what I call Millennial Rules. Pick one. Pick two. Pick three . . . it is a beginning.

The Millennial Rules

Notice that there are not exactly ten Millennial Rules. These are just some of my favorites. You can even supply your own if it makes you happy. The key message is to declare who you are, what you stand for, and share that message with your team. And, la-di-da! Don't be surprised if they share a few of their own!

Consider implementing the Millennial Rules as part of your training program for new employees. That's right—you, acting as the boss-as-parent will need to teach values along with your product and procedure training.

As the saying goes, "Even when the ears are closed to advice, the eyes are open to example." In any kind of training the learner needs to have a visible standard of excellence to serve as a reference point. If you are the boss you are also the visible standard. Make sure you are a visible standard of excellence.

Where do you start? You begin by making values training a company-wide exercise.

So fire up your imagination and create traditions and ceremonies to help anchor those values and experiences you want your team to exhibit. Keep in mind that personal values are anchored by the music and ceremony of one's youth. In an environment where positive values are not celebrated, it's going to be difficult to change hearts and minds. So listen to positive music and frequently celebrate positive behavior.

Millennial Rule: Be-do-have

This is the rule for getting what you want out of life. Instead of waiting for what you want to have to fall into your lap, you begin by deciding to *be* the kind of person who might have what you want to have. Then you *do* the things necessary to *have* what you want.

For example, if you want to have a nice house, begin by deciding to *be* the owner of a nice house. Then *do*; begin doing things that are consistent with having a nice house, which might include treating your apartment as if you owned it. It might mean you will do things at work that could earn you a higher pay. *Be* an owner; *do* the things owners do, and you will eventually *have* a nice house. *Be–do–have*.

If you want to be successful, it helps to look successful. If you want to be successful, do things successful people do and eventually you will have the things successful people have. Do people who are successful in your industry smoke? Show up without shaving? Dress in poorly fitting clothes with rude graphics? If the answer is no, well, you know what to do.

Are people who use illegal drugs or abuse alcohol more or less likely to show up on time, fresh, and ready to work? I rest my case. So the guy who parties into the night and then shows up late or not at all . . . is that the guy most likely to own his own business? Not even!

Millennial Rule: No vs. not yet

Maturity is an important trait that seems to have turned up missing in the Millennial generation. Maturity is the ability to delay self-gratification. For a generation known for entitlement, maturity is in short demand when it comes to smart money management. Notice the upswing in payday loan stores. We've started to notice commercials that even tell younger customers that they *deserve* whatever holds their current interest.

This Millennial Rule is simple. Smart people don't have to get good at saying no as long as they become expert at saying not yet.

More than a few marriages have crashed on the rocks of financial immaturity because of too much yes and not enough not yet.

Millennial Rule: You can't win on a losing team

This would be so obvious if we limited this statement to familiar teams. You know, teams with names or cool jerseys. Well, we all play on teams.

You and your circle of friends form a team. Are you playing with winners or are you on a losing team? Are you leading the team or are you being led? Either way, it would certainly be helpful if someone at least had a plan. Do you really want to wake up far from where you wanted to go?

Marriage is the epitome of a team. Just as values and experiences determine a generation, values and experiences form the foundation of our relationships. With choosing a partner, these values and experiences become even more important when children become part of the family structure. Sadly, in marriage, you aren't going to win if you have signed onto a losing team.

At work, the team you play with has a huge influence on your personal success. Look around and you will notice that in most work settings there is more than one team doing similar work. There may be a day shift and a night shift. You may work for a company with multiple stores, or branches, or divisions. Does it matter which of those teams you work with? You bet it does!

The bottom line is once you have decided your team is a losing team, leave. Change teams!

> I walked into a convenience store and wandered down the nearest aisle. Walking toward me was a shirt-less young man with a scruffy, greasy beard. He was barefoot, as was a woman who entered behind me. She could have easily been his twin.
>
> "Where's your old lady?"
>
> "She's in jail," he answered, without lowering his voice one iota.
>
> "Oh," said the glamorous babe.

Do we need a quiz here? Take a closer look at the exchange between the two shoppers. Obviously they knew each other, and obviously they shared similar values of personal grooming and public appearance. And apparently they have similar values when it comes to following society's rules. "Where's your old lady?" "She's in jail."

Admittedly, most of my readers don't know me other than through reading this book, but if you were to ask me, "Where's Buns?" I guarantee that if I answered, "She's in jail," you wouldn't respond by simply saying, "Oh"!

Try not to be judgmental, but tell me—is it possible that one or both of these folks are losers? And what are the odds that the partners they are married to or, more likely, simply living with, are losers? You make the call!

Millennial Rule: Do the right thing . . . always

Doing the right thing is not always easy. Sometimes doing the right thing can actually be painful. But doing the right thing is always the right thing.

I couldn't see her but I could hear her—the unmistakable clip/scrape of metal crutches on concrete sidewalks I had heard a hundred times before. I knew that somewhere inside a tangle of misshapen legs and aluminum braces was a young girl trying to make the best of the worst, pushing through the crowd of impatient high school students.

I couldn't see her because two of our senior football stars were in front of me, blocking the view.

When I realized what was happening I was sick to my stomach and frightened at the same instant. "Hey, baby," then a taunt about looking good in a bikini now that school was almost out for summer vacation. "Hey, baby," then a cruel tease about making out with them at the local drive-in. "Hey, baby," and I don't recall either the category or content of the next cutting remark. Without thinking about right and wrong, I jumped onto the back of the nearest moron and, well, let's just say, 'got the living crap beat out of me that day' . . . but it sure felt good.

Millennial Rule: If it was easy everybody would be doing it

It is normal, even desirable to want the most out of life. But wanting wealth doesn't bring you wealth. Doing brings wealth. If you want more, you must do more. And keep in mind that the value you deliver is what will determine the value of your reward.

You see, there really is no free lunch. Getting ahead in life takes work . . . and lots of it. And that's good because not everyone will invest the effort.

"Dad?"

The voice on the other end of the phone was our son Rod, who has an uncanny ability to detect when I am not listening . One again, I was busted. Rod gets irritated when I don't listen. (Cursive note to self: pay attention, dummy! He's your son!)

"Dad? I've decided to open my own business. Can you help me look for a location?"

"Sure! I can help this coming weekend."

"That's too late. I am opening in two weeks." Being the good dad that I wish I were, I launched into all the reasons why that just wasn't going to happen. But the twenty-two years of enthusiasm calling from San Antonio had it all figured out. Two weeks till grand opening and that was all she wrote.

Over the next two weeks the calls came regularly mostly to say, "Dad! You aren't going to believe what they (the city) are making me do . . ." followed by me saying, "That's great, son! If it was easy everybody would be doing it!"

On the fourteenth day Rod's Stereo Sounds opened for business.

Six months later an article appeared in the local newspaper, a half page with a headline that read, "County's Youngest Entrepreneur" with a photo of our son standing in front of his sound wall, hands on hips, and a caption beneath the photo that read, "If it was easy everybody would be doing it."

Dad strikes again!

Millennial Rule: Dress, speak, and act like the man who writes the checks

When I accepted my first corporate job, if I had any sense at all, my first stop should have been at Men's Wearhouse. I would have whipped out my credit card and bought myself a suit. Maybe not an expensive suit, but something that would have helped me look like I might belong to the group of executives I had been invited to join.

It would have been overkill to have made my second stop the local BMW dealer, but it would have been a good idea if I had found something affordable to replace my Honda motorcycle. Do you think it stood out parked in the executive parking lot?

I'm not saying that you should not be yourself. On the other hand, if you are radically different, it might be wise to not wave your differences like a red cape in front of a bull.

I am willing to bet those "differences" cost me tens of thousands of dollars over the years.

Millennial Rule: Be a lifelong learner

No matter how smart you feel when you complete your education, keep in mind that change can leave you looking and feeling stupid. Sometimes it seems that nothing stays the same. Your only defense is to be a lifelong learner and learn something new every day.

Millennial Rule: It is up to you, not fate. Win or lose, it is a choice . . . your choice

The following story illustrates this point best.

> I decided to surprise my client and conspired with the food and beverage manager to outfit me in a waiter's uniform to work the break preceding my keynote address.
>
> The break went fine. That's not the story.
>
> The story belongs to a pretty young server wearing a nametag that said Desiree.

"Desiree. That's a pretty name. Is that French? What does it mean in English?"

"It is French," she answered as she looked at her feet and said, "It means the awaited one." Then it took her a second to say, "And who are you?"

"My name is Scott. It means 'he who hardly works!'"

You would have thought that I had hit her with a board. Her head whipped around, as she said, "Does it really?"—more an exclamation than a question.

"No, but why the reaction?"

"Oh, nothing." She looked down at her feet, retreating to wherever young women go when they feel hurt. "It's just that my fiancé is named Scott . . . and he hardly works. I thought you were talking about him."

"I see." This was my best facilitator's routine. Wait patiently. Don't rush to fill the silence. Let the silence fill itself.

"Ever since he moved in, he just goes fishing with his buddies. Sometimes he does things for his friends but not too often. Mostly he just lays around the house, waiting for me to come home and cook dinner."

"Let me guess. You think this will change when you are married."

"Won't it? Won't he want to get a job and save for a house and, you know?" I knew. I really knew and the answer was n-o.

"Desiree, I hate to tell you this but what you see is what you get." She looked at her feet again, which up until this point had been getting most of the attention in this conversation. "Do you mind if I ask you why you want to marry this guy?"

"He's the only one who asked," she said, as if her saying no to this character would have been a sentence to lifelong spinsterhood.

"Quick quiz. Do you think about him constantly? Can you hardly wait to see him when you get home? Are you bursting with pride when he goes to see your family? Okay, I can tell by your response that your answers are no, no, and no.

"Look, I have a son your age so I could easily be your dad. Do you mind hearing from your dad for just a minute?"

"No."

"You are not 'in love' because if you were, you would be thinking about your fellow all day. You wouldn't be able to wait to see him at the end of the day, and you would be parading him everywhere. Think about your Scott and ask yourself if this is how you want to spend the next thirty or forty years, because, trust me, he isn't going to change."

She could barely look up. I knew that I had hit the mark and that it hurt. I felt sorry but knew she had to hear these words.

"Has anyone, even your Scott, mentioned that you are a charming, attractive, young woman?" (No answer.)

"Well, you are. And I'm sure there are thousands of men who would be proud to call you their wife. Now what are you going to do with that?"

Before she could answer, the doors to the meeting room burst open and out poured my audience for their break. Desiree and I worked side by side, playing with the folks as we served up sodas and fun. She had quite a flair for entertaining. All she needed was a partner who would encourage her.

When the crowd began to shuffle back to the meeting room, I knew it was time to clean up and head for my real work. As I tore off my apron and started to say my good-byes, a tall, charming, attractive, and now smiling young woman swept to my side and took my arm. She put her face close to mine so that there would be no missing her words: "Thank you. I made an important decision today. Thanks, Dad!"

She hugged me briefly and I handed her my apron and waiter's coat, hoping that she had indeed gotten more from me than dirty laundry. You can never really know about these things, you can only hope.

Life is indeed a matter of choices. Some of us are lucky. Some of us are smart. Some of us just plain out-work the other guy. You can choose a life on the couch . . . that's your call. Me? I say play hard or go home. I want to fly like my tail is on fire. I want to grab every new day and squeeze it for all it is worth. Carpe Diem!

And here's one more, my favorite . . . *have fun and make the world a better place*!

NOTES

1. Neil Charness, "The Age-Ability-Productivity Paradox," *AARP*, n.d., http://assets.aarp.org/www.aarp.org_/articles/international/CharnessPPT.pdf.

2. Stacie Severs, "An Amazonian Sized Challenge: The Smartpone and Tablet Price Check Era," *The BIG Consumer Blog*, February 9, 2012, http://bigconsumerblog.wordpress.com/2012/02/09/an-amazonian-sized-challenge-the-smartphone-and-tablet-price-check-era/.

3. Jessica Dickler, "Boomerang Kids: 85% of College Grads Move Home," *CNNMoney*, November 15, 2010, http://money.cnn.com/2010/10/14/pf/boomerang_kids_move_home/index.htm.

4. Jessica Godofsky, Cliff Zukin, and Carl Van Horn, "Unfulfilled Expectations: Recent College Graduates Struggle in a Troubled Economy," *Work Trends*, May 2011, www.heldrich.rutgers.edu/sites/default/files/content/Work_Trends_May_2011.pdf.

5. Sharon Jayson, "30% in US Have Never Married, Census Says," *USA Today*, May 19, 2011, http://yourlife.usatoday.com/sex-relationships/marriage/story/2011/05/30-in-US-have-never-married-Census-says/47309028/1.

6. Alex Sundby, "Customer Service Leaves Buyers Irked, Survey Says," *Econwatch*, June 7, 2011, www.cbsnews.com/8301-503983_162-20069669.html#lxzz1PBAJxbRC.

7. Bureau of Labor Statistics, "Labor Force Statistics From the Current Population," *United States Department of Labor*, n.d., www.bls.gov/cps/.

8. Don Tapscott, *Grown Up Digital: The Rise of the Net Generation* (New York: McGraw-Hill, 1998).

9. Tapscott, *Grown Up Digital*, 43.

10. Glenn Engler, "Retreat From Social Media Backfires on Carnival After Italy Ship Disaster," *Advertising Age*, February 14, 2012, http://adage.com/article/digitalnext/post-disaster-retreat-social-media-backfires-carnival/232723/.

11. Terry Blount, "Brad Keselowski Strikes Twitter Gold," *ESPN*, March 2, 2012, http://sports.yahoo.com/nascar/news?slug=jp-passan_brad_keselowski_twitter_022812.

12. Marianne Kolbasuk McGee, "YouTube Videos Stir Up New Sales for 'Will It Blend' Maker," *InformationWeek*, September 27, 2007, www.informationweek.com/news/202102372.

13. Hiscox, "Hiscox Examines Social Media Usage by Small Businesses," *Hiscox*, July 14, 2011, www.hiscoxusa.com/small-business-insurance/newsroom/press/2011/hiscox-examines-social-media-usage-by-small-businesses/.

14. Dave Johnson, "5 Surprising Social Media Statistics That Affect Your Business," *CBS News*, October 11, 2011, www.cbsnews.com/8301-505143_162-28652590/5-surprising-social-media-statistics-that-affect-your-business/?tag=mncol;lst;1.

15. Grant McCracken, "How Ford Got Social Marketing Right," *Harvard Business Review*, January 7, 2010, www.businessweek.com/managing/content/jan2010/ca2010018_445530.htm.

16. Sundby, "Customer Service Leaves Buyers Irked."

17. J.D. Power and Associates. "2010 US Small Business Banking Satisfaction Study," *J.D. Power and Associates* video, 2:14, October 27, 2010, www.jdpower.com/content/video-article/V4k9ryE/2010-u-s-small-business-banking-satisfaction-study.htm.

18. Bureau of Labor Statistics, "Labor Force Statistics."

19. Richard Conniff, "Drones Are Ready for Takeoff," *Smithsonian*, June 2011, www.smithsonianmag.com/science-nature/Drones-are-Ready-for-Takeoff.html.

BIBLIOGRAPHY

BIGinsight™. *Media Behaviors & Influence Study*. Worthington, OH: Prosper Business Development, 2011.

Burbary, Ken. "Facebook Demographics Revisited—2011 Statistics." *Web Business by Ken Burbary*, March 7, 2011. Accessed March 14, 2012. www.kenburbary.com/2011/03/facebook-demographics -revisited-2011-statistics-2/.

Bureau of Labor Statistics. "Labor Force Statistics From the Current Population." *United States Department of Labor*, n.d. Accessed March 13, 2012. www.bls.gov/cps/.

Blount, Terry. "Brad Keselowski Strikes Twitter Gold." *ESPN*, March 2, 2012. Accessed March 13, 2012. http://espn.go.com/racing /nascar/cup/story/_/id/7637627nascar-brad-keselowski-strikes- twitter-gold.

Charness, Neil. "The Age-Ability-Productivity Paradox." *AARP*, n.d. Accessed March 15, 2012. http://assets.aarp.org/www.aarp.org _/articles/international/CharnessPPT.pdf.

Conniff, Richard. "Drones Are Ready for Takeoff." *Smithsonian*, June 2011. Accessed March 13, 2012. www.smithsonianmag.com /science-nature/Drones-are-Ready-for-Takeoff.html.

Dickler, Jessica. "Boomerang Kids: 85% of College Grads Move Home." *CNNMoney*, November 15, 2010. Accessed March 13, 2012. http://money.cnn.com/2010/10/14/pf/boomerang _kids_move_home/index.htm.

Engler, Glenn. "Retreat From Social Media Backfires on Carnival After Italy Ship Disaster." *Advertising Age*, February 14, 2012. Accessed March 13, 2012. http://adage.com/article/digitalnext /post-disaster-retreat-social-media-backfires-carnival/232723/.

Godofsky, Jessica, Cliff Zukin, and Carl Van Horn. "Unfulfilled Expectations: Recent College Graduates Struggle in a Troubled Economy." *Work Trends*, May 2011. Accessed March 15, 2012. www.heldrich.rutgers.edu/sites/default/files/content/Work _Trends_May_2011.pdf.

"Grammy Awards: Record of the Year." *Rock on the Net*, 2012. Accessed March 15, 2012. www.rockonthenet.com/grammy/record.htm.

Gross, T. Scott. *When Customers Talk: Turn What They Tell You Into Sales*. Chicago: Dearborn Trade, 2005.

"Headlines That Shaped History." *USA Today*, September 14, 2007. Accessed March 15, 2012. www.usatoday.com/news/top25-headlines.htm.

Hiscox. "Hiscox Examines Social Media Usage by Small Businesses." *Hiscox*, July 14, 2011. Accessed March 13, 2012. www.hiscoxusa.com/small-business-insurance/newsroom/press/2011/hiscox-examines-social-media-usage-by-small-businesses/.

Jayson, Sharon. "30% in US Have Never Married, Census Says." *USA Today*, May 19, 2011. Accessed May 19, 2011. http://yourlife.usatoday.com/sex-relationships/marriage/story/2011/05/30-in-US-have-never-married-Census-says/47309028/1.

J.D. Power and Associates. "2010 US Small Business Banking Satisfaction Study." *J.D. Power and Associates* video, 2:14. October 27, 2010. www.jdpower.com/content/video-article/V4k9ryE/2010-u-s-small-business-banking-satisfaction-study.htm.

Johnson, Dave. "5 Surprising Social Media Statistics That Affect Your Business." *CBS News*, October 11, 2011. Accessed March 13, 2012. www.cbsnews.com/8301-505143_162-28652590/5-surprising-social-media-statistics-that-affect-your-business/?tag=mncol;lst;1.

McCracken, Grant. "How Ford Got Social Marketing Right." *Harvard Business Review*, January 7, 2010. Accessed March 13, 2012. www.businessweek.com/managing/content/jan2010/ca2010018_445530.htm.

McGee, Marianne Kolbasuk. "YouTube Videos Stir Up New Sales for 'Will It Blend' Maker." *InformationWeek*, September 27, 2007. Accessed March 13, 2012. www.informationweek.com/news/202102372.

"News and Events on This Day in History." *The People History*, 2012. Accessed March 15, 2012. www.thepeoplehistory.com/this-day-in-history.html.

Pew Research Center. *Millennials: A Portrait of Generation Next.* Washington, DC: Pew Research Center, 2010. Accessed March 14, 2012. http://pewsocialtrends.org/files/2010/10/millennials -confident-connected-open-to-change.pdf.

"Public's Top Stories of the Decade—9/11 and Katrina." *Pew Research Center,* December 30, 2010. Accessed March 15, 2012. http://pewresearch.org/pubs/1841/publics-top -news-stories-2001-2010-september-11-katrina.

Severs, Stacie. "An Amazonian Sized Challenge: The Smartpone and Tablet Price Check Era." *The BIG Consumer Blog,* February 9, 2012. Accessed March 13, 2012. http://bigconsumerblog .wordpress.com/2012/02/09/an-amazonian-sized-challenge -the-smartphone-and-tablet-price-check-era/.

Sundby, Alex. "Customer Service Leaves Buyers Irked, Survey Says." *Econwatch,* June 7, 2011. Accessed March 13, 2012. www.cbsnews.com/8301-503983_162-20069669.html #lxzz1PBAJxbRC.

Tapscott, Don. *Grown Up Digital: The Rise of the Net Generation.* New York: McGraw-Hill, 1998.

"TIME's Person of the Year, From 1927 to 2011." *TIME,* 2012. Accessed March 15, 2012. www.time.com/time/interactive /0,31813,1681791,00.html.

"Timeline of United States Inventions (After 1991)." *Wikipedia,* 2012. Accessed March 15, 2012. http://en.wikipedia.org /wiki/Timeline_of_United_States_inventions_(1946%E2 %80%931991).

"Timeline of United States Inventions (1946–1991)." *Wikipedia,* 2012. Accessed March 15, 2012. http://en.wikipedia.org /wiki/Timeline_of_United_States_inventions_(1946%E2 %80%931991).

"The Top Story Index." *Pew Research Center,* 2012. Accessed March 15, 2012. http://pewresearch.org/databank/newsindex/.

INDEX

A

advancement, 119
Advertising Age, 61
Amazon.com, 5, 62, 79
American Express, 65
attitudes and beliefs, 116–120
avatars, 126–128

B

Bank of America, 24
Beird, M., 88
BIGinsight, 5, 45
Boomers, defined, 11
Boot City, 94–95
BrainX.com, 115,
Bridge Generation, 18

C

Carnival Cruise Corp., 61
CBS News, 39
Cialdini, R., 54
cluster technology, 45
cohort, 16
collaboration, 108–109
communication methods
See also online
communication; social
media
generational comparison of,
17
compensation, 118
competition, 117,
complaints, handling, 98–100
Conniff, R., 128

Costa Concordia, 61
Costco, 86
Covey, S., 73
credit card debt, 34
customer service
See also digital consumers;
Positively Outrageous
Service (POS)
changes in, 3, 21–22
complaints, handling, 98–99
critical points, 88–90
defined, 91
expectations, 25–31
future of, 129–130
importance of, 91
influence of Millennials on,
37–41
instantaneous, 25, 88
negotiation, role of, 25–26
social media, role of, 24–25
technology, role of, 22–24
unbundled, 28–29, 86–88
customization, mass, 29–31

D

decision making, 118–119
delivery options, 27, 84
digital consumers
See also customer service
development of, 11–12
dos and don'ts list, 35–36
Dodge.com, 62
Domino's, 62
dress codes, 116
Durkin, T., iii, 65

E

ease and convenience, 89
employees
    future of, 126–129
    Millennials as, 105–111
Engler, G., 61
execution, 117
expectations
    customer service and,
      26–31
    technology and, 60–61

F

Facebook, 67, 74
Fast Company, 79
FedEx, 38
Ferrara, J., 68–69
Five Guys, 29
Forbes.com, 72
Ford Motor Co., 70
FourSquare, 56, 63
freedom of choice, 109–110

G

Gage, R., 23
Garcia, M., 105
generation(s)
    communication methods,
      comparison of, 17
    defined, 12, 16–19
    timeline, 13–15
Generation X, defined, 11, 16
Generation Y. See Millennials
Ghag, S., 74–75
Gladwell, M., 67
GoldMine, 69
Google, 62

Go Social, 56, 63
gossip, 1019
Grown Up Digital (Tapscott), 60

H

hiring
    Millennials, 105–111, 118
    questions to ask, 114
    values, understanding new,
      107–111
    home, Millennials' attitudes
      toward, 33–35
home ownership, 40
humor, use of, 101, 109

I

Influence, the Psychology of
    Persuasion (Cialdini), 54
innovation, 117
instantaneous delivery of
    services, 25, 46

J

J.D. Power and Associates, 87

K

Karol, C., 97
Klein, B., 48

L

Lady Gaga, 19, 79,
leisure time, 32
Letterman, D., 88
Live Community, 70

M

Marcus, M., 38
marketing

expectations and, 60–61
invisibility of, 60
networks, 62–63
social media for, 73–77
traditional, 63–65
marriage, 34
mass customization, 29–31
McDaniel, J., 97
McNeill, C., 75–76, 96
McQuaig Job Survey®, 113–114
media, influence of various, 64
Millennials
defined, 11, 17
description of, 21–41
labeling, 20
Money.CNN.com, 33
Monster.com, 34
motivation, 86
music, 12, 13–15
MyCyberTwin, 127–128

N

National Oceanographic
and Atmospheric
Administration, Office of
Diversity, 16
National Speakers Association
(NSA), 19
negotiation, role of, 25–26, 85–86
Net Gen, 60
networks, 62–63
Nimble, 62, 69

O

online communication,
importance of, 61–62
online purchasing
delivery options, 84

negotiation, use of, 85–86
online research
delivery options, 84
methods used, 4–5, 82–83
prepurchase, 81–83

P

People History Blog, 16
performance, 115–116, 118,
120
Pew Research, 16
Positively Outrageous Service
(POS)
customer complaints,
handling, 98–100
defined, 5, 91–92
humor, use of, 100–101
surprise and examples of,
93–98
Positively Outrageous Service
(Gross), 5
price, value and, 89
purchasing. See online
purchasing

Q

Quickbooks, 70

R

Rack Space, 32
research. See online research
River's Edge, 96
Robbins, T., 23
rockonthenet.com, 16
Rutgers University, 33

S

Saeks, F., 23

salespeople
    changing views toward, 27
    friendly and knowledgeable,
       89–90
    Millennials as, 105–110
Sam's Club, 86
selling
    authority/believability, 56
    comfort/convenience,
       56–57
    consistency, 57–58
    contrast, 55
    desirability/affinity, 56
    engagement, 57
    invisible, 45–48
    positive feelings, creating,
       54–58
    reciprocity, 48
    scarcity/exclusivity, 55–56
    surprise, 58
selling process, FUSE
    execute, 51–52, 99
    friending, 49, 45–46, 99
    online, 52–53
    solve, 50–51, 46, 99
    uncover, 50, 46, 99
Service Prescription, The, 38
Sims, J., 51
Sitel, Inc., 71, 105
Smith, R., 98
Smithsonian, 128
social media
    marketing with, 73–77
    power of, 69–72
    role of, 24–25, 67–69, 82
    tips for using, 77–78
    users of, 68

Soft Puppy close, 27
Sony, 74–75
Southwest Airlines, 28–29,
    66–68, 85–86, 89
Sundance Film Festival, 60
surprise, use of, 93–98

T

tangibilizing, 87
Tapscott, D., 60
technology
    cluster, 45
    expectations and, 60–61
    invisibility and, 60
    networks, 63–64
    role of, 22–24, 59
    timeline, 13–15
Technorati, 62
texting, 24–25
Time, 34
time.com, 16
Tipping Point, The (Gladwell), 67
Toyota, 56
Traditionals, defined, 11, 17–18
training
    attitudes and beliefs,
       116–119
    importance of, 103–105
    just-in-time or matrix, 40
    Millennials, 114–119
trend spotting, 4
TwentySomething.com, 33
Twitter, 67, 73–74

U

unbundled services, 28–30,
    87–88
USA Today, 16

V

value, adding, 29, 89, 117
Vang, F., 6, 27, 41, 45, 47, 49,
      53, 54, 73, 92, 94, 98,
      100, 103

W

Wagner, B., 113
waiting, 88
When Customers Talk (Gross),
      5, 45
Wikipedia, 16, 36

Wolf, D., 56, 57
work
      changing world of, 125–131
      ethics/lifestyle, 118
      Millennials' attitudes
      toward, 31–33 , 108–110,
      115–119

Z

Zakos, J., 127
Zappos, 32
Ziglar, Z., 23

ABOUT THE AUTHOR

T. Scott Gross is more than a writer who speaks; he literally has been there and done that!

A veteran of the hospitality industry, audiences everywhere respect Gross as an entrepreneur who knows what it is like to make payroll every Friday.

Best known for his first book, *Positively Outrageous Service*, now in its second edition, sold worldwide in a multitude of languages, Scott continues to delight audiences with his subtle humor, masterful storytelling, and take-home value, challenging them to make work fun. His subsequent books, fourteen in all, validate the need—and rewards—of delivering a customer service experience so positive that your customers become your best marketing tool.

Scott's client list is as diverse as the Fortune 500, including such respected companies as Southwest Airlines, Ford, and Walmart. Presenting to audiences from as small as six to more than three thousand, Scott has chosen to hone his skills in more diverse territories. He has served as a First Responder (EMT-B) in his small community of Kerrville, where he recently completed his third term as a city council member. When not on the road, Scott intends to live life to its fullest, always making a difference!

Books from Allworth Press

Allworth Press is an imprint of Skyhorse Publishing, Inc. Selected titles are listed below.

From Idea to Exit: The Entrepreneurial Journey
by Jeffrey Weber (6 x 9, 272 pages, paperback, $19.95)

Peak Business Performance Under Pressure
by Bill Driscoll (6 x 9, 224 pages, paperback, $19.95)

Intentional Leadership: 12 Lenses for Focusing Strengths, Managing Weaknesses, and Achieving Your Purpose
by Jane A. G. Kise (7 x 10, 200 pages, paperback, $19.95)

Emotional Branding, Revised Edition: The New Paradigm for Connecting Brands to People
by Marc Gobe (6 x 9, 344 pages, paperback, $19.95)

Brand Thinking and Other Noble Pursuits
by Debbie Millman (6 x 9, 320 pages, paperback, $19.95)

The Art of Digital Branding, Revised Edition
by Ian Cocoran (6 x 9, 272 pages, paperback, $19.95)

Infectious: How to Connect Deeply and Unleash the Energetic Leader Within
by Achim Nowak (6 x 9, 256 pages, paperback, $19.95)

Rebuilding the Brand: How Harley-Davidson Became King of the Road
by Clyde Fessler (6 x 9, 128 pages, paperback, $14.95)

The Art of Digital Branding, Revised Edition
by Ian Cocoran (6 x 9, 272 pages, paperback, $19.95)

Corporate Creativity: Developing an Innovative Organization
by Thomas Lockwood and Thomas Walton (6 x 9, 256 pages, paperback, $24.95)

The Pocket Small Business Owner's Guide to Building Your Business
by Kevin Devine (5 ¼ x 8 ¼, 256 pages, paperback, $14.95)

The Pocket Small Business Owner's Guide to Business Plans
by Brian Hill and Dee Power (5 ½ x 8 ¼, 224 pages, paperback, $14.95)

The Pocket Small Business Owner's Guide to Negotiating
by Kevin Devine (5 ½ x 8 ¼, 224 pages, paperback, $14.95)

To see our complete catalog or to order online, please visit *www.allworth.com*.